M000097198

CONFESSIONS OF A REPEAT OFFENDER

Musings on a Life Gone Right in Spite of Myself

By: Phillip Giambri
The Ancient Mariner

Printed in the United States of America.

First Printing, 2016

ISBN-13: 978-0692607244
www.Createspace.com
www.AncientMarinerTales.com

Cover Art by Linda Wulkan

Dedicated to all the Barflies and Broken Angels with whom I've spent the past fifty-five years sharing Happy Hours, love, four AM closings, loss, booze, hope, cigarettes, creativity, bar stools, dreams, Slim Jims, and life stories. I wouldn't trade a minute for a million.

Introduction

My first glimpse at becoming a writer is in seventh grade. I surprise my teachers, my parents, and myself by winning an English class writing award for a brilliant autobiography covering my entire thirteen years - of what seems at the time, an interesting and dramatic life. Watch out Hemingway!

In 10th grade, my English teacher tells my parents that he feels I should be thinking about a career in writing. Having just hit puberty, I'm smoking unfiltered Chesterfield Kings, drinking Seagram's 7 daily, and fantasizing what a woman's breasts will actually feel like, after seeing a topless picture of Sofia Loren in the first issue of Playboy magazine. Writing is put on the back burner by a constant erection that I'm hoping might offer more exciting opportunities. It doesn't.

In the military, there's a daily ship's newspaper where I write anonymous stories, transposed from popular movies, of daily peculiar incidents that my shipmates are involved in during long periods at sea. They're popular, but I never consider them anything more than junk food and a cool distraction from my unhappy military life. The ship's Weapons Officer, also a writer for the newspaper, repeatedly suggests that my attention might best be directed toward writing, rather than my apparent pursuit of becoming an early-death alcoholic. I briefly consider it, but dismiss it as yet another father figure trying to grow me up. I have no intention of growing up, and feverishly pursue my hell bent mission of self-destruction.

In spite of my attempts to continue down the road to an early and glorious death, I leave the military, and somehow wangle a scholarship to an acting school, where I'm also the editor of the school's newspaper. This damned writing muse seems determined to not let me escape her clutches for some reason.

After graduation, I move to New York and spend ten years working in theatre, in just about every capacity except playwriting, while writing a monthly column for our block association newsletter.

None of these writing events ever seems anything more than a temporary distractions from my intended descent into an early alcohol and drug induced shuffle off the mortal coil.

Sidetracked through several more careers, I abandon writing and evade early death, until I become engaged in a virulent letter writing campaign to prevent being fired from a job. I'm continually in trouble for voicing objections to the way my coworkers and I are harassed and mistreated. My letter writing proves more plausible to the "powers that be" than the lies of our superiors, and the writing blitz leads to a dismissal of charges against me. I'm offered a better position in a different department, where my technical writing skills are honed and come to the forefront.

Two years later, I'm offered a prestigious job with a new employer and at the age of sixty-five, I end my full time work life in the last of at least twenty different "careers." I'm working as a consultant technical writer for an IT Department in a major hospital, where I had spent more than ten years as an IT Network Manager.

Retiring fully from the working world, I'm finally in a position to complete my long sought dream of holy self-destruction, but something's changed. Somewhere along the way, I seem to have unintentionally grown up, and death no longer seems a desirable and romantic goal. It's time for a "Plan B", but what? With time on my hands and nothing to do, I attend readings by local writers and poets. The little writing muse starts whispering in my ear that I can do this, if I actually decide to get serious.

Phillip Giambri may be a fairly accomplished technical writer, but I need to dig deep down inside and find that thirteen-year-old who wrote the humorous autobiography, long ago, when I was still pure and innocent. Months of futile attempts at capturing that youthful innocence, lead to the discovery of a grizzled old creature lurking on the fringes of my consciousness. He's willing and eager to comment on the long track record of misdeeds, mistakes, and misadventures of my reprobate life. He reveals himself to me as The Ancient Mariner, and his voice comes forward and leads me to this, my end-game, writing adventure, "Confessions of A Repeat Offender." I finally commit to becoming an honest writer. I think my muse is very relieved. Her long dark mission seems finally accomplished.

CONTENTS

Chapter I

My Life as a Barfly

It all begins at **Charlie's Log Cabin Inn**

It's the late 1940's,
I'm six or seven years old,
and it's a blistering hot August afternoon.
I'm on my grandmother's back lawn
in rural South Jersey, watching,
as Uncle Leon removes the washboard
from Grandmom's large metal washtub.
He places it carefully against a post
on the side of the back porch.
He lifts one side of the large tub
and tips it over.
A wave of soap and bleach water
foams out across the lawn,
and slowly soaks into the ground.
I watch and wait.
Moments later, big fat night crawlers
start popping up
through the grass and suds,
like magic.
I grab 'em and stash 'em
in a Maxwell House coffee can.
I spread a little dirt on them,
cover it with wax paper,
put a rubber band around the wax paper,
and poke a fork through it,
leaving four tiny holes for air.
I stash the can in the shade under the porch,
to save 'em, for when I go fishing.

Uncle Leon takes my hand, walks me across the lawn,
and down the side of the road about 20 yards.
We pass our neighbor Charlie "The Goat Man's" house.

We cross over the blacktop,
and head down a narrow dirt road,
passing Chicken Yocci's house......
He's the weird neighbor
that all the kids are afraid of.
I push in close to Uncle Leon's leg
and hold his hand tight, as we pass,
hoping Chicken Yocci won't put the *Maloccio* on me.

We cut through an opening in a split rail fence,
encircling a lawn,
with a long, low, log cabin in the center.
There are old wagon wheels,
propped up with sticks on the lawn.
It looks like a stagecoach stop
in a John Wayne western movie.
As we get closer to the cabin door,
a small neon sign flashes "Charlie's Log Cabin Inn."
Uncle Leon pushes open the heavy wooden door ....
I'm wild with excitement and have no idea,
that I'm about to fall down the rabbit hole forever.

The darkness blinds me for a moment,
but I feel the cool air of the room on my cheeks...
there's the smell of cigarette smoke, ashtrays, beer, and peanuts.
I hear a Phillies game on the radio.
Eddie Waitkus is on second,
Richie Ashburn hits a homer and ties up the game.

As my eyes slowly adjust,
I can make out a dim light over a circular bar,
in a large open room,
with hot beams of intense sunlight,
shooting across the floor from tiny windows.
There's some booths in the back, a jukebox, a shuffle board,

a cigarette machine by the door,
and a pinball machine against the front wall.
It's an old Gottlieb machine
with Lil' Abner and Daisy Mae
painted on the glass,
and Daisy May is wearin'
a really low cut, tight fittin' blouse.

My uncle picks me up,
sits me up on the bar, and pulls up a stool.
He orders a coke for me and a beer for himself.
He winks at me,
and we share the knowing smiles,
of two pals on "road trip."
He pops a stick match with his thumbnail,
lights up,
and takes a long slow draw on a Lucky Strike,
while the barkeep draws his beer.

The bartender yells over,
"Hey kid, what's your name?"
I shyly answer, "Phillip."
He comes back from the register,
hands Uncle Leon the beer,
and offers me a handful of nickels
painted with red nail polish.
"Ever play pinball, Phillip?"

My face lights up like a neon sign.
I nod a silent "Yeah," yell a quick "Thanks,"
and leap from the bar,
one hand full of red nickels,
the other full of peanuts,
arms pushed up high in the air,
I make a mad dash for Daisy Mae,

wearin' a shit-eatin' grin,
wider than the Grand Canyon....

For me, that moment remains frozen in time
forever.
I knew I was home.

Johnny Boy

If the Internet was around in 1955
and you could Google Juvenile Delinquent,
Johnny Boy's name and picture
would definitely pop up first.

Johnny Boy is my sister's boyfriend.
He's the best looking, most athletic,
and most evil person I've ever met.
He's 6'2", blonde haired, blue eyed,
and heavily muscled for a teenager.
He's Marlon Brando, James Dean, and Elvis…
all rolled up in one really bad-ass Greaser.

Every girl in the neighborhood is in love with him,
and every guy is scared shitless of him.
 We all want to be him, be like him,
or at least, be around him.

I'm allowed to hang around him
only because of my sister.
I do shit jobs for him
 just so I can tag along with the older guys;
I'm a freshman; they're juniors….
In high school, that's a big deal.

Johnny Boy's parents never seem to be home.
He regularly has card games in his mom's kitchen.
I run for cigarettes and coffee.
I also mix drinks for them from bottles of Seagram's Seven
that Johnny Boy and I liberate from the local bar.

He conveniently leaves a cellar door unlocked
when he delivers kegs of beer

for his father's beer distributing business.
On our way out,
we grab handfuls of quarters from the cash register,
for the poker game.

Johnny Boy and his buddies play poker for quarters,
while I mix 7&7s for them,
sneaking sips from the bottle,
until I get really drunk.

Johnny Boy is walking me around the neighborhood
trying to sober me up.
We stroll through the commuter-train parking lot.
He keeps tryin' out car doors,
until he finds one that's open.
He slides in behind the wheel of a black '49 Chevy hardtop.

He's gonna hot wire the ignition
with silver foil he tears off,
from the top of his pack of Lucky Strikes.
He reaches under the dashboard,
and jams the silver foil
into the back of the ignition,
shorting out the contacts.
I watch and learn.
He presses the starter button,
the engine kicks over,
and we head out toward US 1.
Johnny Boy looks over at me
with that cool badboy grin,
and says, "We're goin' to Miami."
I'm really scared
but really excited too.

I say nothing.

I nod my head, force a smile,
and light up an unfiltered Chesterfield King.
I'm tryin' to act cool,
like I do this shit all the time.
It's dark in the car,
so I'm hoping Johnny Boy doesn't notice
how much my hands are shaking.

In Maryland,
we pick up a hitchhiker
who calls himself "Radar."
He gets to ride shotgun now,
and I'm moved to the cramped back seat.
Radar and Johnny Boy talk a lot.
Radar is nineteen,
been in prison, and has a gun.
He and Johnny Boy seem to have a lot in common.
I feel myself slowly becoming invisible.

We stop for gas in Virginia.
The gas jockey asks for the gas cap key.
Without hesitating,
Johnny Boy gets out of the car,
walks casually back to the gas cap and easily twists it off,
breaking the lock.
He flashes an innocent altar boy smile
and gets back in the car with the gas cap.
The teenage attendant doesn't say a word,
but is clearly impressed.
Chalk up another victim to Johnny Boy's charm.

We speed out of the station
streaming a trail of gasoline
from the open gas tank.
I'm hoping Johnny Boy

doesn't flip his cigarette butt
out the open window.

Around midnight,
we're deep in South Carolina,
with Radar driving.
He pulls off the road, into the woods,
and we sleep in the car `til sunup.

I wake up,
and have to pee real bad.
I get out of the car
and walk into the woods a bit.
I hear the engine start.
I turn around quick,
and see the rear wheels sliding,
and kicking up wet leaves.
Johnny Boy and Radar drive off.

At first I think they're only messing with me,
but after an hour, I get it…
they're not coming back.
I'm scared.
I'm fourteen,
in the middle of nowhere,
with no money,
my stomach's growling,
I'm out of cigarettes,
and my mouth tastes like ass.
I'm fucked.

I finally hitch a ride very late in the morning.
I give the driver a sad story
about how the last guy
that picked me up,

took my money and left me in the woods.
I don't know if he really believes me,
but he's a nice guy and he buys me a meal.

I doze off,
and fourteen hours later,
he amazingly drops me off in Pennsylvania,
not far from where we started.

Meanwhile, my father
had me declared a "chronic run-away."
I have a date in court later in the week.

The judge asks me
why I continually run away from home,
I sneer out, "My father's too cheap to take us on vacation."
….which is mostly true.
The judge gives me a slap on the wrist.
My father is embarrassed and really pissed off.
I'm grounded. Big time!

Jump ahead two years
to my last adventure with Johnny Boy:
He's bashing in the rear door of a bar,
at night, with a tire iron.
I'm lookout.
He's not subtle. It's noisy.
Somebody calls the cops.
Johnny Boy runs a lot faster than I do.

I don't rat him out,
and that costs me a night in jail,
a beating by my father,
six months' probation,
and I lose my driver's license for a year.

I'm expecting at least a grateful wink or nod
next he comes over to pick up my sister,
but he just points his finger at me
and laughs his ass off,
with that same charming,
innocent, schoolboy look.
He's really a sick fuck.

My mother's been charmed by Johnny Boy,
for a long time.
She only makes my sister break up with him,
when he goes to prison for a two-year stretch.

I'm hoping he gets to share a cell
with some hardcore lifer
who's so charmed by that smile,
that he makes him his bitch.

Dive Bars

I've spent the best years of my life in dive bars.
There's still a few good ones left in the East Village,
but they'll all be gone before long
thanks to high rents, hipster invasion, and organic yogurt spots

When I moved to New York in 1967,
I was amazed to find
there was an actual franchised chain of dive bars.
They were called Blarney Stone,
and they were as common
as Starbucks are now.
They catered to blue collar workers, alcoholic housewives, sailors,
construction workers, bike messengers, hookers,
pimps, old drunks, white collar executives who didn't want coworkers
to see them bangin' down six martinis for lunch,
and out of work actors like me.

There's actually one remaining Blarney Stone,
on Eighth Avenue across from Penn Station.
I spent a lot of hours in that one back in '61 and '62,
passing through the city when I was in the service.

They had steam tables with mashed potatoes, string beans
and the best corned beef, roast beef,
and roast pork sandwiches in the city.
You could always get away with the excuse
that you were stopping by Blarney Stone
to get a corned beef sandwich
and then get smashed in the middle of the day,
'cause what really brought the hard core,
afternoon drunks to Blarney Stone,
was the cheap booze;
ounce and a half shots of bottom shelf shit.

What is now politely called "well drinks."
$.25 a shot with a coke chaser,
or $.35 a shot with a short beer chaser.
Every hour was Happy Hour at Blarney Stone.

I like to think I'm more sophisticated now;
I enjoy the taste of single malt scotches,
California wines, French brandy, and aged bourbon;
mostly when somebody else is buying, of course.

But I gotta tell ya, I still have nostalgia
for Old Philadelphia, Corby's,
Schenley's, and Three Feathers;
cheap shit, that bites at the back of your throat
and lets your stomach know
that something bad is comin' down.
Whenever I think back on good times,
when I think of good friends,
all my best memories seem imprinted
with the smell, the taste, and the bite,
of bottom shelf whiskey in dive bars.

It makes me feel warm inside.
I wish I were young again,
and still had a stomach
that could handle cheap booze.

The Meaning of Existence

Two dirt encrusted old winos
with broken faces,
sitting on the window ledge
of the vitamin store
on First Ave @ 14th
sharing a bottle in a bag,
bummin' smokes from passersby,
and discussing
the "meaning of existence."

Considering their current situation,
I'm thinkin' they might not
have really found the answer yet,
but I guess it's good
that they're workin' on it.

Playing Picasso

It's late.
I'm sittin' alone at the bar,
working on my fourth
double Jack.
I'm feeling pretty mellow.

She leans across two seats,
taps me on the shoulder,
stares me dead in the face,
and slurs out,
"You look like Pablo Picasso."

She's really pretty.
I'd guess late thirties,
or early forties, maybe,
sculpted cheekbones,
and a great body,
packed into tight black leather.
Her hair is long and straight
and dyed black,
with bangs, almost covering
those haunted, crazy eyes.
Exactly the woman
I've always been a sucker for!

"Pablo Picasso! Yeah!
 I bet you get that all the time, huh?"

"No, not really."

She spots my fancy camera
sitting on the bar.
"Hey, you're a photographer?"

I say, "Sometimes.
But mostly, I tell stories."

She flashes a wide wasted grin,
"Hey, me too!"
and she drifts off
into some rambling drug story,
with a couple of lame attempts
at being funny.

I say, "Ya know, everything you say,
seems to have a sardonic twist
of some kind,
like a comedian, or something."

She smiles suggestively.
"Well…I am a comedian."

"Really?
What kind of comedy do you do?"

She says, "Da Da."

A "Da Da" comedian?
(Really?
Could she be that hip?)

She asks, "What kind of comedy do you do?"

I repeat, "I'm not a comic,
I tell stories."

She coyly replies, "Well,
I'm sure that my stories
are a lot more interesting than yours!"

22

as she slowly moves
her face and lips
up very close . . . .
to an attack position.

"Hey, I've got a Speedo at home that's older than you!"

She dusts me off, saying,
"You couldn't come close to my stories.
Have you ever done crack?"

"No, I stopped
at Mescaline and Coke.
You obviously didn't. …"

She again ignores my comment and asks,
"What comedians do you like?"

"I don't know…Richard Pryor and Lenny Bruce,
Andy Kauffman, Sarah Silverman …"

"Wow!
Ya' know, everybody thinks
 I *am* Sarah Silverman."

"Really? I can see that."
(In a dark bar, with enough drinks,
she actually could pass for Sarah Silverman.)

 "And Andy Kaufman is my hero,
my role model."

She rests her hand on my thigh.
My Cialis instantly kicks in,
telling my body
that I'm 40 years old again,

while Jack Daniels agrees,
and is whispering in my head,
"Go for it, man! You can do it!"

She's seems pretty intelligent,
somewhat creative,
attractive,
very sexy,
and very fucked up.
Just my kinda' girl!
I offer her my card
and invite her
to my next show.

(Why do they still entice me;
these beautiful, intelligent, crazies?
And why do they still seek me out?
Do they see the leftover crazy
in these old eyes,
past the wrinkles
and the beat up face?

Shouldn't she be able
to see in me,
that it doesn't work?
I'm living proof.
I have the scars
of battles lost
with "crazy"
"drugs"
and "booze."

"But more important,
why do I feel this incredible emotional
and sexual magnetism here?

It's an old feeling
that I sure miss.
It feels good!
Is it just the Cialis
and the Jack Daniels;
purely a chemical reaction?
I don't think so.")

I know better!
But still....
I want to throw her on the back
of a `60 Triumph Bonneville
race off to some cheap motel
and make hard bandit love to her.
We're crazy.
That's what we do, ain't it?
Feel bad tomorrow, right?

(We're both losers ya' know,
headin'
for a "Bonnie and Clyde" ending here;
Pablo Picasso?
Sarah Silverman?
Two fucked up souls,
irreversibly drivin'
into a head on, dead on, collision.)

She leans in and hugs me,
way too tight.
I feel myself wanting
a lot more,
but ya' know,
age sometimes
actually produces
bits of wisdom.

I grab my camera
and head for the door;

I hear her yelling behind me,
"Hey Pablo,
why are ya' leavin', man?"

I've been
in this same sad movie,
way too many times.
I'm not gonna hang around
for the bad ending anymore.

Cheap Shots

Most days I feel like
I'm dream-walking
through a life that's a graveyard.

Ghost voices
from all the bars
I ever hung out in
call out to me,
to come home.

I know
I belong with them
there;
yet I struggle to exist
in the real world.

I've spent a lifetime
faking it
and do what I have to do
to keep it together.
I'm really good at it
but, they're still calling me.

In some dark corner of my soul
I know I was born
to be there,
with them,
destined to sit alone
forever......on a stool
at the far end
of some dive bar.

Somehow I escaped.
and managed
to have a real life
for a while,
thanks to a woman

27

who cared enough
to love me
in spite of myself.

She's gone now
and they're still out there...
waiting for me
to come back.
I used to think I could escape
for good
but I know it's my real home,
the only place
I've ever really belonged.

I feel like I'm destined
to spend eternity
in a broken down
bus station bar,
in some shit hole city,
drinking bottom shelf rotgut,
feeling lonely and sad,
and wishing for the life
I already have.

Night Troll

I am your night Troll,
crumpled, old, and invisible.
By day confined to a writer's cave
for fear of embarrassment.

I am the online fantasy
of that tall handsome Latin lover
your heart seeks as the answer
to lonely hungers.

You indulge me
and offer your soul
to this Cyrano in hiding,
but light of day
offers only professional equality,
and shared intellect
with guilt of need for Troll attention.

Hearts lay in silent wait
for the return of lonely night
and shared make-believe,
when the Troll emerges once again
to fulfill your online fantasy
as white horse knight of your dreams.

Are You Dangerous?

She registers with this online dating site,
fills out the forms, and posts a picture.
Within minutes, she gets a text response,
from some guy who says he likes her nose.
She doesn't respond.

Moments later he texts again,
asking, "Are you dangerous?"
She doesn't respond.

A few minutes pass,
and he sends her a dick pic.
A real romantic we got here, huh?
In what universe is that supposed to be some kinda turn on?
He has no idea at all who he's dealing with here.
Let's take it back to the "Are you dangerous?" question for a minute:

It's Sunday afternoon and she's sitting alone
at the far end of the bar.
She's chattin' up my buddy the bartender.
I come in and take a seat at the opposite end.
The joint's empty except for the two of us.
I'm sittin' there for like five minutes
watching her bat her eyes at my buddy.
He seems oblivious to my presence.

I clear my throat a couple of times,
then fake a loud cough,
finally extracting him from her talons.
 He strolls over and mixes up my "usual."

We pick up exactly where we left off last Sunday;
The typical barfly bullshit conversation.
She's eavesdropping

30

and later tells me she knew immediately that:
A) I'm someone who wouldn't notice or remember her,
and
B) I'm someone whose skin she definitely wants to get under.

Part "A" not true;
I don't make a habit of starting conversations
with strangers drinking alone
in an empty bar on a Sunday afternoon;
I figure they might be needin' some space.

But what the fuck?
Let the games begin!
She opens with Bukowski: Do I like him?
It becomes very apparent very quickly
that whatever I reply
will be immediately rebutted
with a deliberately opposite opinion.
"Devil's Advocate?"
I'm thinkin' more like "Happy Hour" ballbuster.
So, Part "B" true!
Someone *is* getting under my skin.
She pisses me off;
mission accomplished.
I respond in kind.

You know how you get dog shit on your shoe
and you can't seem to shake it off?
Well, call it fate or destiny,
but I keep running into her
at all my favorite joints.
She's on me
like a pit bull that won't let go.
She challenges everything I say,

BUT...
what begins as a confrontational dual of wits,
slowly and imperceptibly grows,
into fascination, interest, respect, and finally,
a challenging and enduring friendship,
flavored with Happy Hour whiskey,
and lots of stimulating conversation.
.

Again, to the point, "Is she dangerous?"
I'm thinkin' on this,
watching,
as she inhales long and slow,
on that American Spirit menthol,
her idle hand taps softly on the bar;
A dirge of broken hearts,
false starts,
and roads goin' nowhere.

So, if dangerous means tangling
with some sexy, smart, lady,
who can go shot for shot with you,
while fucking with your head,
and you're still likin' it ......
then yeah;
she's dangerous,
very fucking dangerous.
…….. and I like her nose, too.

Nobody Wants to Get Crazy Anymore

I don't know exactly when,
or what the fuck happened,
but nobody
wants to get crazy anymore.
Nobody seems
to have the need
to blow off some steam
and scream!

After a couple weeks
of tryin' to be "normal"
I need to get crazy,
if only for a couple hours,
just to stay sane.

All my "Get Crazy" friends
keep gettin' married,
gettin' sober,
gettin' religion,
gettin' in rehab,
gettin' in shape,
or gettin' dead.

I partied my way
through four generations
of "Get Crazy" friends,
but I keep losin' `em
to real life.

Nobody wants to get crazy anymore.
What the fuck?

Inertia Eve

Inertia: *"The tendency of a body in motion to remain in motion."*
She oozes the seductive scent of Salome,
with body moves,
as flexible as a Russian gymnast.
She is the temptress Delilah;
armed and ready to shear.
(Thank god I don't any have hair!)

She approaches slowly
like a stalking panther,
with the hypnotic stare of a snake charmer's cobra;
body ever swaying side to side,
in a perpetual fluid motion.
She defines inertia!

Taking the seat beside me at the bar,
the room is suddenly showered with pheromones,
like butterflies emerging from a warm cocoon.
Every man at the bar picks up the scent,
and feels hunted, stalked,
and becomes preoccupied
with the thought of having her.

Every woman snaps to attention.
A gauntlet has been thrown down.
There is the sticky sweet smell
of blatant competition,
swirling in their midst.
Cold stares over crossed arms,
and sad, stern looks of resentment,
only add
to the heavy sexual tension
in the room.

She converses,
not so much with words,
but with gestures,
and casual touches,
and soft caresses.
I'm wary,
but intrigued, fascinated, and totally immersed,
in the pheromone frenzy she's created
around our little corner of the bar.

Conversation requires few words.
Our minds spark an electric shock connection,
revealing a oneness of thought, emotion,
and experiences mutually shared.
There is a likeness of spirit and will,
that overshadows even the heavy sexuality.

Thoughts and feelings pass between us,
that have remained largely unshared until now.
We know that we are brother and sister,
of that same cosmic mother,
share the same imprisoned soul.

She is the incarnate female version,
of the troubled, joyous, intellectual demon
that was me,
on my journey of self-destruction
those many eons ago.
For Eve in the garden,
there is only one possible endgame
to this tangled, strange, encounter:
consummation.
The fakir's charmed serpent,
offers up the forbidden fruit.

This bar: "The Garden."
The onlookers: "The Almighty," (who will judge),
and I: the decaying remnant of that very first Man,
am to decide the outcome,
of this timeless invitation.

The apple has been offered.
Adam must decide,
if binding vows
previously spoken,
will now be broken;
Truly a conundrum of biblical proportion!

A Toast to Johnny E

You could always find Johnny E
in the last seat,
at the end of the bar,
for Happy Hour at The International,
over on 1st Ave near 7th street.

"Three fingers Bushmills.....neat."
Always "dressed to the nines"
with a carefully arranged
and shellacked "comb-over,"
and wearing that classic
powder blue, polyester sport coat
he got thirty-five years ago
back in `72
on his way home from "Nam."

"Hey Johnny E,
haven't seen ya' for a while. Where ya' been?"

"Aggghhh, the fuckin' ambulance
took me to Emergency at Bellevue,
instead of the VA Hospital.
Eight weeks there with pneumonia,
and they tell me I got a bad liver
to boot."

"Goddammed landlord
rents out my apartment
to a woman with a kid.
`Cause he hasn't heard from me,
he thinks I'm dead.
Thirty-five years of my life
he throws in a fuckin' dumpster."

"Then my car's missing.
I go down to the tow pound.
They auctioned off my car
for $75 bucks.
They said I owed $2,300 in
tow charges, fines ,
and storage fees."

"I got $468 in my savings account.
I'm runnin' outa' fuckin' options here, ya' know?"

He spends "happy hours" at
The International for a few more weeks until his stash runs out,
just tryin' to stay warm
and keep a little buzz goin'.

As the weather gets colder,
panhandlin' ain't workin' for him anymore.
When I run into him again,
he's sleepin' on a heat vent
by the Chase bank on 2nd Avenue.
I spot him a twenty and ask,
"Hey, Johnny E, how's it goin'?"

"Rejoice, rejoice, we got no choice….right?
Maybe I need to try the VA again, huh?
I was a door gunner on a Huey back in Nam, ya' know?
Company A, 1st Battalion, 35th Infantry,
I lit up a lot of VC with that big 50', man!
No retreat, no surrender!
Fuckin' "A" brother!
They owe us somethin'. Right?"

I don't see Johnny any more that winter;
on the street
or at The International.

Late one night
I'm over at the Black & White on 10th Street,
shootin' the shit with Harry "The Hat,"
and outta' nowhere, he says, *"Hey, remember Johnny E?*
Frankie The Cop tells me,
they found him dead
in a room over at the St. Marks Hotel, back in March.
Yeah, he was face down in a Swanson TV dinner;
Mac & Cheese, I think,
still wearin' that fuckin' polyester sport coat .
Ya know what's sad,
Frankie says nobody claimed his body.
Can ya believe that shit?"

"Hey Billy, three fingers Bushmills….neat!"

"To Johnny E;
No retreat, no surrender!
Fuckin' A brother!"

Dancing on Razor Blades

Late night East village.
Rain glistens off sidewalks
like shattered glass.
Crazy lookin' couple roamin' the streets:
Long leg beauty in full length leather
takin' long strides in black cowboy boots
blonde hair blowin' wild, open coat, denim mini skirt,
and Ramones' T-shirt pushin' out hard nipples,
draggin' along some BoHo old hipster
sportin' a black porkpie hat, and Chuck Taylor high-tops,
lookin' for all the world like some sexy '60s
"truckin'" cartoon couple.

Coyotes stalking Alphabet City,
hungry for the taste of pre-gentrification.
Looking to bite off and chew up
the last remaining conversation
on music, poetry, love, and art
lingering in dive bars
still open
to poets, rockers, artists, and crazies.

A broken wing angel
and a poet out of rhyme,
"Jukin" the East Village Dive bars:
Drink a little, dance a little,
Make out at the bar,
not carin' who's lookin',
feelin' the music
feelin' the love.

Hit the street again,
on the prowl,
hungry for the next joint.

They keep rollin' on,
bar after bar
'til there ain't no more, left;
drinkin' too much,
talkin' shit,
laughin' too loud
groping under street lights,
refusing to submit to daylight
ever.

They're dancin' on razor blades,
taste freedom in the blood.
Their time is passin' fast and they know it.
Soon there'll be nowhere left to go
for poets, rockers, artists, and crazies.

Fuck burning candles at both ends,
douse 'em in gasoline,
turn up the music,
drink, smoke, laugh, love.
Let the flames be your final sunset
'cause baby, we got nothin' left to lose now!

A Blonde, A BoHo, A Broken Bed, and Bodega Beer

Saturday night East Village:
Long "Happy Hour" at the local bar.
Fired up on "well drinks,"
Blondie and the Boho
are ready to stalk.

Two coyotes headin' South
prowling the edge of Chinatown
'til they find a joint
with loud music blasting
from a tenement basement.

Grab a couple drinks
and a seat way in the back
suddenly surrounded
by middle-aged Jersey couples,
fat, tired, and worn out,
lookin' to re-live college days.

Ain't long before Blondie and Boho
are jumpin', swayin',
shakin' hair, and shakin' ass,
bodies vibrating to pounding music,
making out and gropin' between drinks.
Jersey couples stare, awkward and nervous,
embarrassed by this shameless couple,
but secretly wishing
that they still had that passion.

Blonde coyote girl
goin' to the bar for refills
bumps their table
spilling drinks.

Jersey couples leave;
Don't even wait to see their band.

Just know they're talkin' shit
about the juvenile behavior
of those two coyotes
doin' what they're doin'
but I'm thinkin'
they're gonna' go home,
jump in the sack,
and for just a few minutes,
try to be coyotes too.
Good luck with that Jack.

Blondie and Boho stay late,
'til the music's all gone,
head back to the East Village gropin',
thinkin' dirty thoughts,
and itchin' for some "play time."

Those two coyotes
gonna' break that damned bed again,
drink warm Bodega beer,
and hug 'til the sun comes up,
'cause that's what ya' do
early Sunday morning, East Village.

East Village Dive Bar New Year's Eve

Late afternoon holiday party
with the usual suspects
and some young Army and Marine vets
who stop by.

Heavily tattooed beauties
cruise hipsters with man buns,
obviously not from around here.
Military guys buying drinks
for this old Mariner.

My buddy and I get feelin' pretty good.
He walks me home at seven
drops to the floor in my apartment,
and cries 'cause his life is falling apart.
I hold him for a moment.
"Happy New Year buddy."
He's off to Bronxville
for a lady who still cares about him
in spite of everything.

We're the East Village dive bar New Year's people
who don't make the morning news.
Asleep before the ball drops
'cause there ain't no reason
to stay alive much longer.
We're the ghosts of New Year's past
and we're dyin' real slow.

The approaching *End Game*
Hard Rain on First Avenue after Midnight

A broke down old drunk man,
stumblin' down First Avenue in the rain,
tryin' hard not to slide away,
held up mostly by his cane.
With his good arm he's supportin' a girl
with a swelled up foot that hurts,
slow steps movin' forward,
then jerkin' and staggerin' back, in spurts.
She's hangin' on tight,
teeth clenched,
fightin' to hold back screams of pain.
She hoists a broke umbrella
strugglin' for cover,
from the rain.

Two poor lost souls,
knowin' they can't do it on their own,
stumblin' down First Avenue together,
tryin' hard,
to find a way back home.

Just a broke down ole' drunk man,
and a pretty young thing in pain,
wandering through purgatory,
in this godforsaken rain.

Chapter II

The Village Idiot

BoHo's Lament
or
Mental Projectile Vomiting is not Politically Correct

"Give me your tired, your poor,
your huddled masses, yearning to be free.
The wretched refuse……………"
Wait…. weren't we all part of that *wretched refuse*?
Weren't we the outcasts, the freaks,
the faggots, the tattooed rockers,
the weirdos, nerds, and techno-geeks,
from all those puckered-ass towns,
in the middle of America,
where we were bullied,
ridiculed, and beat up?

We came here, to The Village,
immigrants from that other America,
seeking refuge,
freedom to let out the crazy creative shit inside.

What happened?
This was The Village;
Bohemia, home of free thought!
When did we submit to politically correct?
We let Giuliani and Bloomberg
sucker us into becoming part of
The Great "I Love NY" Theme Park!

Is anything here left to experience for real?
Washington Square Park
has been cleaned up and made pristine,
and Tompkins Square Park
is a playground for kids and dogs.
They don't want you there anymore,

drinking and smoking weed!
The East Village has been "gentrified"
so be careful, behave yourself.

Little Italy?
Mean Street? Gangsters? Bookies? Social Clubs, Mafia?
……. all gone.
Nothing left but a couple of tourist trap restaurants
and some fake festivals….. swallowed up whole by Chinatown.

Times Square…… is Madame Tussaud's Wax Museum,
The Lion King, and "I love NY" T-shirts.
The Flea Circus is gone.
The $1.00 hot dogs and midnight triple feature movies are gone.
The religious soapbox crazies and Harlem hustlers are gone.
The sleazy jerk-off peeps are gone,
dive bars, "tranny" hookers, and "loose joints"… all gone!

Where do we get the provender,
for new stories, new adventures?
Manhattan was always scary,
but it was real, and it was exciting.
It fed the veins of generations of art junkies.

The Village? …. It's just another stop
on the Grey Line bus tour now.
We've all become
background "extras"
for the daily deluge of tour buses,
TV and film crews.
They invade over our neighborhood,
trying to "package" our environment,
hoping to add some "local color" and excitement,
to their bland, "made for middle-America"
TV shows and movies.

Art? It's video junk food,
made for those same assholes and bullies,
we left behind
in Shit City, USA.

Now we're safely contained
and declawed like zoo animals.
They gawk at us as they ride by
on their double decker tour buses;
or we enter their homes
safely locked up and caged,
as "background" images on their wide screen, High Def TVs.
Our silent submission, gives them permission,
to look down on us, and feel superior.

A Village bookstore hosts an open mic,
where performers are requested,
to not speak five specific four-letter words,
because they might scare off paying customers.
If words scare you,
maybe you should stay the fuck out of book stores.
Your children shout out these same words
every day
on their Christian and Orthodox school buses.
We hear them!
Didn't George Carlin win that fight for us
a long time ago?

This is The Village! If you don't like it,
go back to Yonkers, or Oyster Bay,
or wherever the fuck you come from,
where your smiling, genteel neighbors
are probably whispering those very same words
about you, behind your back.

What happened to:
hang out, drink cheap wine and talk about art;
stumbling out of The White Horse Tavern at 2am,
smelling wino piss and garbage
on hot August sidewalks,
wanting desperately
to follow in the literary footsteps of
O'Neil, Thomas, Kerouac, Ginsberg, Feiffer,
Dylan, Mailer, Hamill,
Cummings, Corso, Ferlinghetti,
and all those other immigrant vagabonds
who painted portraits with words,
of the America we wanted to live in?

I want to write poems
on a midnight fire escape
under moonlight;
I want to make fast intense love
in a dark tenement doorway,
while a "Loisaida" fighting cock,
heralds in the sunrise;
I want to sing the song of my life,
to the world,
with a guitar,
on a park bench;
I want to get wild, get creative, get crazy,
get arrested, get high.
I just want to feel alive again!

Fuck it! Why don't we all
just dress up like Beatniks, Hippies, and Punks,
take pictures with the tourists,
and be done with it!
Welcome to the I Love NY Theme Park!

The Shower

A lady disrobes
Bathrobe cast aside
Cautiously steps into shower
Daring the spray of cool water
Enveloping her warm body
Forcing her body awake
Giving a shock of cold
Hot knob turned for balance
Igniting a blend of pleasure
Just temperate enough to
Keep tingling body sensations
Longing for more warmth
Moaning for more sensation
Nurturing a feeling in a sensitive body
Offering a spray of unexpected sensations
Privately assigned to erotic areas
Quickly raising the tempo of body movement
Raising body temperature and movement
Stimulating unspoken softness
Towards an electrifying ending
Unequaled in sensory privation
Visiting previously unexplored and untouched
With a pulsating pounding causing
Xtasy and release ….
Yes, yes, yes, yes, …….. in body
Zones previously untouched by this pleasure.

Open Mic for the Disenfranchised

I'm an Open Mic Gypsy.
We're the wannabees
the almost famous,
the has-been famous,
and the never gonna be famous.
We're the next wave,
the new wave,
and for some of us,
this is an endless wave.

We'll show up for the opening of a new bodega,
if you give us five minutes and a microphone.
Open Mic is our training wheels, our mistress, and our sirens call.

Who are we?
We're the aging Mulberry St. Guinea comic,
whose jokes now mock
the Guido, Sopranos, Jersey Shore, Wife-beater T –shirt,
image of himself
he so carefully constructed and played out,
for most of his life.

We're that radical Swarthmore Lesbo
who chooses to protest now
without words or signs,
displaying her flawless porcelain body,
in burlesque reviews,
that ridicule our obsession
with fame and sexuality,
while titillating
male tourists' imaginations
with the possibility
of wonders

that will never be.

We're the English Lit PhD,
bullied by the kids on his block,
for being an *uppity nigga*, too smart for his own damned good!
Now he's relentlessly rappin' and slammin' his truths on open mic,
with no apologies, no regrets,
and in your fucking face, *brother*.

We're the second generation freckled Mick,
singing songs of rebellion and anarchy
to comrades in an Irish homeland
that only seems real now
on a drunken St. Paddy's Day.

We're the skateboarding middle class Jap kid,
who grew up on The Beatles and rock and roll
and wants to put his own stamp on our music,
but he's gotta work in his mom's sushi joint
until that happens.

We're the lapsed Catholic, ex-altar boy,
too damaged for any real relationship,
whose poems cry out his loss of faith,
after being irreverently probed,
as a child,
by his parish priest.

We're the self-educated beaner busboy
studying English and writing poems,
on a park bench,
who dreams in vain
of becoming a real waiter,
and replacing that pretty white girl,
who smiles enticingly at him

while stealing part of
their shared tips to feed her habit.

We're the Afghan war burnout
who traded bullets and IEDs
for shots of heroin and Jameson,
to ease the pain,
while writing diaries
of a love lost in Ohio,
and drifting off into
combat nightmares
at AA meetings.

We're the gifted Israeli artist,
who, unmarried, unapologetic,
and rejected by her community
for the crime of being single and female at forty,
now blesses the locals here,
with tattoos of exquisite beauty,
and joyous songs of new love.

We're that drop-out fag college student
from Levittown,
who didn't fit his parent's expectations
of who he was supposed to be,
but who fits perfectly
into a slinky lamé cocktail gown and stilettos
for his standup routine,
and turns tricks on the side,
for more money
than his father makes in a month.

We're the Hassidic Jew boy
who dropped acid, trekked the Himalayas,
and became a Buddhist monk,

spilling out saffron wrapped poems
of beauty and oneness,
on street corners,
to passersby
who will not listen.

We're the pimple faced kid from the 'burbs
escaping a boring tedious life,
popping Oxy from her mom's medicine cabinet
until she leaves home to sing her story here.

We're that retired Camera Guy,
whose head is so full of words,
and rhymes, and ideas, and metaphors,
that they're literally spilling out of his brain
as spontaneous improvised Spoken Word
while his body dances in a hypnotic rhythm.
"Oh babies!"
We're the Nuyorican street boy,
from Avenue B,
who graffitis his way into showings
at prominent Village galleries,
raps his shit on open mic,
and gets to fuck
a beautiful blond white girl
from Minneapolis,
which is all he ever really wanted.

We're all here, downtown,
in The Village, on Open Mic.
The line in the sand is 14th Street,
cross it, and ya takes yer chances,
'cause you're in our world now!

Chapter III

Salty Sea Stories

My Spy

She's stunningly beautiful.
She tells me her name is Anastasiya.
I ask her why she's here.
She smiles seductively but doesn't answer.

We're on a dinner cruise out of Southampton, England;
Two hundred fifty ex-submariners from twenty countries,
gathering every year to reminisce and party.
The weather is chilled and windy,
so we're below deck, swilling down free wine.
I'm working on my second bottle.
I'm feelin' pretty damned good.

I'm seated with a middle aged Russian couple,
a Turkish national,
a drunken, fat, bald, old Russian,
who looks like he's always sweating,
a Turkish American friend,
and my New York buddy, Michael.
We're drinking heavily and chatting loudly in fractured English
with lots of broad, wine induced, hand gestures.

I find myself side glancing
at a blond, blue-eyed woman,
probably in her early fifties,
sitting diagonally across from me, at the next table.
Beside her is a mature good looking man.
She's chatting with an attractive dark haired woman
sitting across from her.
Looking for an excuse to check her out,
I first take pictures of the crew at my table,
then go over to her table,
and gesture for her
to snuggle in close to her husband

for a photograph.
She replies in nearly perfect English
that he is not her husband
but rather the husband of the woman
sitting opposite her.

Great news!
I hand over my camera
and ask her to take a picture of me
with the dark haired wife.
She does.
Then I take a picture of her,
with the lady's husband.
(The camera loves her face.)

I ask her what connection she has with submarines.
She replies that her father was an Admiral in the Russian navy.
(This means a privileged upbringing
in the upper echelons of Russian society.)
But that really didn't answer my question.
I ask again what her connection is with submarines,
and why she's here with us.
She smiles suggestively but doesn't answer.

Back at my table,
I continue chatting with my mates,
while frequently glancing over at her.
She avoids eye contact,
but I catch her staring at me on side glances.
The game plan, is to begin a conversation
with the gentleman next to her.
I ask if she'd be kind enough to translate for us.
She agrees.

As fate would have it,
he's a retired Russian submarine captain,
whose sub was operating
in the same patrol areas as my submarine,
in the same time period, during the Cold War.
We both have a good laugh
when he reminds me how loud his submarine was
compared to our quiet American boats.
We bond our shared memories with a big Russian Bear hug.

The blonde is suddenly interested in me.
She offers her hand and tells me her name is Anastasiya,
and that she's a tour guide in Moscow.
Her English is almost flawless,
with just an intriguing hint of an accent.
Dizzy from too much wine,
I feel myself getting sucked into a dark hole.
Why am I obsessed with this woman?

We exchange business cards
and she studies mine carefully,
commenting that she likes the picture
of me on the back, performing on mic.
We take several close photographs together
and I swagger back to my table,
feeling cocky as hell.
My table mates have been eavesdropping.
Through wine thickened lips,
the Turk, the Russian wife, and my American buddy
all slur out that "she is not to be trusted!
If she's really the daughter of a Russian Admiral,
she would never associate with a tattooed, old, American sailor."

"Hey, that's bullshit.
The Russian women all love to have their pictures

taken with me and my tattoos.
Remember in Greece last year,
Vlad asked me to take off my shirt
in that restaurant by the Acropolis,
so he could photograph tattooed me,
with his Barbi-doll trophy wife?
Fuck yeah! The Ruskies love me!"

They laugh loudly at my bravado, but still insist
that she's a Russian government agent
and is not to be trusted.
"A fuckin' spy? KGB? Come on!"
What fifty year old secrets could I reveal
that would be relevant today?"
My buddy Michael replies,
"Then she's probably looking for a Green Card
and a free ticket to the States."
I'm a bit more wary now, but still intrigued.
"Hey come on guys, she's so fuckin' beautiful!"

Later, I'm shooting videos
of everyone dancing to oldies.
She's right there in front of the camera
shimmying and shaking her ass to "Hound Dog."
She has a great body.
Suddenly, I'm very aware that my Cialis is working.

Back home,
I receive a Facebook friend request,
from her.
I accept.
She messages me,
asking if I remember her from the dinner cruise.
"Remember you? How could I ever forget you?" I reply.
She asks if I would send her copies

of the "excellent pictures," she knows I took of her.
I do,
I also send along that video
of her dancing and shaking her ass.
She replies that, "The pictures are of great quality.
Thank you. I hope to hear again from you, very soon."

"Hope to hear from me again very soon?"
I'm sure she's just fuckin' with me now.
She's gotta' be a Pisces;
I'm a Leo and they just love to mess with Leo's heads.

I check her Facebook page.
There's more than a few of my fellow submariners,
from the convention,
trying to hook up with her,
showering her page,
with romantically embellished words,
in mostly bad and broken English.
I'm definitely not that guy.

I know she's toying with me in these emails,
It's a cat and mouse game.
I reply, "I'm very much looking forward
to seeing you again
at the Saint Petersburg convention.
Perhaps you could arrange a private tour?"
The ball is in her court now.

Spy or not, she's good,
really good.
But this ain't my first rodeo either.

Rosie's Wool Knickers

It's the early 1960's, the height of the Cold War. I'm in the Navy, assigned to a nuclear missile submarine. We regularly deploy off the coast of Russia…. just in case they decide to start World War III. We're part of a Strategic Deterrent Force and, in the event of a missile attack on the United States, we will retaliate by firing our missiles in a brilliantly cynical plan called *Mutually Assured Destruction,* or *MAD.* Does anybody see the irony here?

When not waiting for orders to *"end the world as we know it,"* I'm usually hangin' out at the bar of the Crown Hotel, in Dunoon, a resort town on the banks of Holy Loch, in Scotland. It's known mainly for building the world's fastest racing yachts, and for the annual Highland Games, where tall muscular Scotsmen, wearing traditional kilts, gather to hurl telephone pole sized logs great distances. Needless to say, lots of single Scottish school teachers traditionally spend their summers here looking for husbands, a summer fling, or perhaps just a peek under those manly kilts.

We're the first American servicemen stationed in Scotland since World War II and we're welcomed like Royalty, by everyone, especially young women. I'm in daily competition with my shipmates for the attention of the local girls. I'm also heavily involved in an unofficial competition for the title Town Drunk, for which I seem to possess an uncanny natural propensity.

Across the Loch from Dunoon lies the town of Greenock. As a demonstration of their high regard for the "returning Yanks," the kind folks of Greenock, in a ceremony at their Town Hall, graciously decide to formally adopt our entire crew! A chamber music group is playing, and the mayor is dressed in top hat and tails for the presentation. We're seated at ornately decorated banquet tables, and feasting on prime Angus steaks and champagne. Our Captain is presented with an original Scottish Tartan, designed specifically to honor the "Polaris Missile Program," and our crew in particular. A magnificent event, marred only by loudness and excessive drinking, by myself and more than a few of my shipmates. Later, stumbling down the street, I realize that I have to take a leak that's not gonna wait. I stagger into a doorway, desperately trying to unbutton all thirteen buttons of my uniform pants. Just as I begin to relieve myself, I look up and see that the door has a full length glass center, and everyone in a Tea Shop is staring at me.

Following that incident, I think maybe I shouldn't go back to Greenock for a while, so I start taking the ferry up to Gourick, about an hour across the Loch from Dunoon. I'm polishing up my drunk act at the first bar I find, and somehow, I hook up with Rosie.

Rosie's in her late twenties, good looking, in a hard kinda way that I like, and looks like she's been around the block a few times. She's very petite, with sharp penetrating eyes. She laughs easily and really loud, and has the same sick, cynical sense of humor as me. This is gotta be a match made in hell. We become the drinking, partying, and always too-loud attraction, wherever we go. Everybody seems to know and like Rosie, but we're not allowed in lots of places. For what I assume, is because of my Neanderthal behavior, we're excluded from most social functions in town...with the exception of bars, so mostly we hang out and drink with Rosie's friends. I have no idea where Rosie lives and never think to ask.

Lots of nights, we're drinking and partying 'til very late and I miss the last ferry back to Dunoon. Rosie proves to be really resourceful. At the rail yards, she has a friend who let us sleep on parked trains for the night. She also has a night watchman friend at the local YMCA. He lets us sleep on the floor in the men's room. Sometimes we get woken up by guests coming in to relieve themselves. They always nod politely, carefully step over us, and go about their business, while trying hard not to gawk or laugh at us.

On summer nights, another friend of Rosie's let us stay in the cemetery, where we make love and sleep on cool marble grave covers. Once, a bobby rides by on his bicycle, while Rosie is riding me. He just says, "Hi Rosie!" smiles, and rides on. She yells back... "Hey, Fergus. How's the baby?" she waves, looks down at me, and we continue on. At the time, I'm more concerned with her wool underpants rubbing hard against my inner thighs and burning like hell. Ya know a lot of working class women and "factory girls" in Scotland can only afford wool underwear, 'cause wool's cheap. The country's full of sheep. Rosie wears wool knickers, even in summer. I'm still carrying a few burn scars from those damned knickers.

Picture this now: It's a beautiful sunny Sunday morning; we're strollin' along the promenade heading out of town. My arm is draped over Rosie's shoulder, her arm is around my waist, her hair is up in a beehive, and she's wearing my favorite white polka dot mini dress and high platforms….. she's got great legs! We're laughin', and kissin', and pullin' long swallows from a bottle of scotch. The heather on the side of the hills is shooting glimmering purple starbursts through the morning mist; absolutely beautiful… Life is good, and we're feelin' good.

We stop at one of these photo booths, in the arcade, where you put in a couple of shillings, pull the curtain, and pose for pictures. We finish off the bottle first, put a couple of coins in the machine, and take two rounds of pictures. We're feeling kinda frisky and we sneak in a couple of pretty intimate poses in the second set. While we're waiting for the pictures to come out of the machine, we both nod off. When we finally wake up, God knows how much later, we're half undressed and Rosie's beehive is lookin' like The Leaning Tower of Pisa. We grab the pictures from the machine. In the first set we're huggin' and smiling and lookin' happy, but by the last picture in the second set …… "How the hell did we get in that position in this booth?" What the fuck. ….. Rosie, she looks old. Her breasts are all wrinkled and saggy ……. I look drunk and really stupid. My face is so full of zits, I look like I took a load of buckshot. "Jeeesus, what a reality check!" I tear up the pictures and we head over to the Crown where we can drink until we look beautiful again in the mirror behind the bar.

Once a month, Rosie goes up to "the big city," Glasgow, to visit her grandmother for a long weekend. I stay on my side of the Loch, drinking at the Crown.

Speaking of Glasgow, on my second Cold War Patrol, I complete a very intensive Submarine Qualification training program. When we get back to Holy Loch, my buddies take me up to Glasgow, to the notorious Baresford Lounge, to be initiated into a very elite brotherhood of sailors entitled to wear the Submariners Dolphins insignia.

Out of respect for those of you with weak stomachs, I won't go into the details of the "initiation" ceremony, but I leave The Beresford, totally shitfaced, along with my friend Gary, and two equally drunken hookers. On the way to their "hotel," we're chattin' up the cab driver and convince him to stop and have a few drinks with us. The cabbie gets really drunk and Gary volunteers to drive the remaining couple of blocks to the whorehouse, I mean "hotel." He's had way too much to drink, and never drove on the other side of the street. We bounce our way down the street side-swiping about six cars before we get to the whorehouse. We leave the cabbie laid out in the back seat of the cab, check into the hotel, and proceed to "get it on."

64

Later, I'm relaxin' in bed, while the "lady of the evening" is getting us more drinks. I decide to take a stroll downstairs through the lobby. No one seems to notice or care that I'm really drunk and very naked. Across the lobby, I spot a close friend of Rosie's pouring a glass of wine for some guy. I remember her from a nasty incident in Gourick. I stagger toward her yelling, "Hey.....you stole Mike's radio." She sees me, turns fast, breaks the wine bottle on the edge of a table, and charges, aiming the broken bottle directly at my face. She's cursing at me and laughing like hell, as she chases me over the broken glass, until I'm out of the lobby, and makin' a mad dash for the stairs.

I find Gary's room, knock hard, and I'm yellin' at the door: "Gary....I'm in trouble. We gotta get outta here, now ...." The door opens and there's a huge erection staring up at me. The hooker's standin' behind him smiling, wearing his open peacoat..... Wow! She has nice boobs! He leans into my face and slurs out, "*I ain't leavin' 'til I get laid, again*!" "Gary, it's me, your best friend!" "*You're on your own, pal*!" He slams the door in my face.

I stagger back to my room, fumble into my uniform, and run barefoot down to the train station, carrying my shoes, my coat, and my hat. The last train to Dunoon already left and the station's closed for the night. I toss the night watchman a couple of bills and he lets me sleep on the empty morning train for the remainder of the night.

The train suddenly starts moving and I wake up. For a second, I think I'm almost sober. I look down. My feet are all cut up, covered with dried blood, and burning' like hell. My mouth tastes like ass, my head's exploding, and where in hell are my socks? I catch a glimpse of those shiny new "Dolphins" pinned to my uniform and break into a big, shit-eatin' grin. "Hot Damn, I'm a real Submariner now!" In spite of everything that's happened, this has to be the proudest moment of my life…...

On the train ride back to Dunoon, a realization slowly seeps through the dense fog of this hangover ……… "*ROSIE IS A HOOKER*!" …..…... Of course! How could I not have seen it? That's why we're not allowed in dances and the shops in town. It's not me or the drinking; It's Rosie… she's a whore! Everybody knew but me? ……JEEEESUS!

The Russian fishing fleet anchors near Glasgow every month to resupply. The crews aren't allowed ashore, so prostitutes are brought out to service the men

CONFESSIONS OF A REPEAT OFFENDER

and keep morale up. Rosie can make enough money in one weekend *visiting her grandmother* to live on for the rest of the month. "DAMN, I'm stupid!"

Well, I never go back to Gourick, and I never see Rosie again. She searches for me, in all the bars around Gourick and even Dunoon, but always gets the same line that sailors use to cover for a buddy: *"Giambri? He's on Restriction for disciplinary reasons. He can't leave the ship."* She's very persistent. She repeatedly calls the ship and speaks to the Duty Officer. She pleads with him to let me come ashore. Finally, Commander Douglas, The Executive Officer, calls me to his stateroom and says, *"Giambri, I like to believe that we're running a pretty secure operation here. What I need to know is how a local woman, on a land line, is able to repeatedly place calls to a restricted phone line, on a Top Secret US Navy vessel, asking for you?"*

"Not really sure, Sir, but she does have a lot of friends."

"This stops NOW! Fix it, or it goes higher up."

Well, I can't. I rely on the only option I know when things go wrong; keep on drinking.

That's not quite the end of the story. My friend Steven tells me, he thinks that actually I'm the whore in this story. Rosie was just doing what she had to do, to make a living. It was hard times there. She loved me the best way she knew, and I was the one "using" her. He says, "Who the fuck are you, thinking you were better than her? You were a twenty-one year old punk with a bad attitude, a drinking problem, and a face that looked like a fuckin' pepperoni pizza! What a self-righteous asshole you were!"

He was right, ya know. I wish now, that I'd kept that picture we took hugging in the booth at the arcade, instead of tearing it up, like an eight year old in a tantrum.

These demons from my youth… they still haunt me!

My Wild and Wonderful Weekend with Weegee

It's the summer of 1963, I'm returning to the states from my fourth and last "Cold War" submarine patrol. No more war games, spy games, or waitin' to nuke Russia. In two months, I'm out. I'm gone. I've got a plan: quit drinking, the GI Bill, back to school. .. start writing again, and try to get a real life.

At the duty free shop in Prestwick, Scotland, I'm allowed to purchase, and take back, four Imperial quarts of whiskey; that's a lot more than a gallon of booze. Okay, "The Plan" is on temporary hold. I hit the states and I'm ready to party my ass off.

Doc and I leave New London, Connecticut by train, headed for a weekend in Philly, our hometown. Doc's a lifer in the navy, and about ten years older than me. He's from North Philly; I'm from South Philly. He's black; I'm not. We're not close friends, but we've pulled four long patrols together. We've got each other's back. We know we can handle anything that can happen to two horny sailors, carrying two and a half gallons of Scotch, on a five hour train ride.

We take seats in the last row of the last car, backs against the bathroom wall by the water fountain. The two seats facing us are the only empty seats in the car when the train leaves. Apparently, nobody wants to sit facing two sailors filling paper cups from very large bottles of Scotch. Our "Welcome Home" party is underway.

At the stop in New Haven, two very attractive ladies, who look to be in their mid-twenties, board our car. They're standing in the aisle alongside us, arms folded, staring, and finally ask, *"Would you please move your feet off the seats so we can sit?"* We mumble a lame apology, and they take the seats opposite us. We try to act nonchalant and paste on fake smiles as we continue pouring Scotch and bangin' 'em down.

Meanwhile, across the aisle from us, a loud group of college kids has been watching us pour and consume a lot of whiskey. They ask if we'd mind sharing some. We say, *"Sure!"* They grab a bunch of cups from the water fountain, we fill them, and in short order, the ladies sitting across from us ask, if they too might have a drink. We grab a few more cups, and thus begins our Mission of Mercy: getting everybody on the rear half of our train car, totally smashed, by the time we make Newark. Including the conductor.

We hit New Brunswick and the ladies are way past tipsy. Doc asks one of them to switch seats with him, and she does. Now we're sitting alongside two very nice looking babes. I ask the lady seated next to me what her name is and she giggles out, *"Gwennie, but everybody calls me Weegee."* She giggles again. This is gonna be good.

I'm feeling pretty high, but can't help noticing that she's really sexy. She's got one of those trendy beehive hairdos, ya know, like The Supremes? She has velvet smooth, purple-black skin, and a beautiful face. She's wearing tight fitting dungarees, a way too small tee-shirt, and her breasts look like bumper guards on a '55 Caddy El Dorado.

By the time we reach North Philly station, we've killed three bottles of Scotch, sharing with our neighbors on the train. Doc suddenly jumps up and yells, "Hey, this is my stop! I gotta go!" A drunken chorus of our new friends starts chanting, *"Stay on the train. Don't leave the train,"* stomping their feet, and clapping in rhythm. The ladies chime in and invite us to Chester to continue the party with them. I give Doc a pleading look and he finally says, *"Well, okay. I guess I'm in!"* He sits back down and the kids pour another round of drinks for everybody.

At 30th Street Station, we give a quart of Scotch to the college kids to share with the other passengers, and we leave the train with the ladies, to loud cheers and applause. We board a train for Chester and dazzle the girls with tall tales of life at sea. We are a couple of smooth silver tongued devils.

In the cab heading for Weegee's apartment, I ask her what she does for a living. She says she and Wanda are dancers (I'm thinkin' like, Go-Go Dancers, in a cage, wearing white vinyl knee boots, and miniskirts, like on that TV Show!) Wow! How cool is that?

Weegee and I are snuggled in tight, groping each other in the back seat. I overhear Wanda whispering to Doc, *"What's up with this white boy? What's he doin' hangin' with us?"* Doc says, *"Don't worry. He's alright."* *"Are you sure?"* *"I said he's cool. Drop it."* She does and it never comes up again.

In Weegee's living room, we get ice cubes with our Scotch and the ladies switch to rum and coke. Wanda puts "Dedicated to the One I Love" on the record player. Weegee and I are dancing slow and tight, grinding hips with lots of lip and tongue action. Wanda leans in to Weegee and says, *"Let's show em?"* Weegee looks up at me and whispers, "You're gonna love this." and they leave for the bedroom.

Doc and I bang down a couple more scotches and when the girls finally come out, they're wearing tasseled pasties, tiny sequined G-strings, and platform stilettos. "*Holy shit; they're strippers!*" Doc and I look at each other, dazed, like two weary prospectors who just hit "the mother lode."

Doc and I are sitting on the couch now, and there's a raunchy sax wailin' out Night Train on the record player. The girls are bumpin' and grindin' through their routines, boobs bouncing, tassels whirling like carnival pinwheels, and hips thrusting just inches away from our faces. This has to be as close to heaven as this submarine sailor's ever gonna get.

The combination of Scotch, the music, the erotic dancing, and the heavy scent of perfume, is way too much stimulation. I've just spent sixty days underwater in the North Atlantic, smelling nothing but diesel fumes and ball sweat.

Within milliseconds of the music ending, Weegee and I are both naked on her bed, trying to fill our hands, eyes, mouth, and any other available body parts, with each other. To this day I have never encountered a woman with such a perfect body ….. WOW! ..... We're talkin' Playboy quality here! Yeah, I know, Hugh Hefner can never have a "colored" girl for a centerfold………. but she's hot, she's sweet, she's funny, and I am totally lost in her for the weekend.

We kiss, cuddle, and make love, through an incredible three days and nights, pausing only for food, a quick nap, a smoke, or another drink. It's mostly she and I, discovering how incredible two bodies can make each other feel.

I can't say for sure what caused that magic; it may have been my forced abstinence, her magnetism, or just a strong mutual attraction spiked with lots of booze. Whatever chemistry happened, resulted in a physical stamina that I had never experienced before, and have never again, since. *I was pretty fuckin' amazing* and Weegee seemed to agree, judging by the loud screams and moans she's offering well into day two. From the sounds in the adjoining bedroom, Doc seems to be on his best game too … pretty amazing for an old desperado like him.

Comes Sunday morning, the girls accompany us back to the train station. I do not want to leave…. ever. I give Weegee my address and ask her to write me. We cling to each other in an embrace that neither of us wants to end. Doc finally grabs me by the collar and drags me to the train. We're both stone silent as the train pulls out of the station. We take a long last look at the ladies waving us off. Doc shakes his head and says, "Ain't we just the fuckin' baddest?" We don't say another word 'til we change trains in Philly.

For the next two weeks, all I'm thinking about is Weegee. I'm replaying the weekend, over and over, in my head. Doc says I'm acting like a lovesick puppy and reminds me that *"It was just a weekend thing. We had some fun. That's it! End of story!"*

I have a knot in my stomach until a letter finally arrives. I'm surprised at how excited I am opening it. Weegee says she can't stop thinking about me and wants to move to New London to be with me.   Uh..Oh! That's not what I'm expecting.

The fantasy suddenly takes a hard left, into reality. There's a bright red neon "NO" flashing in my brain now. Do I really have the guts to stand up to my family, my friends, and all the shit that's gonna come down on both of us as a mixed race couple?

While pondering this heavy moral and ethical question, my little "Man Voice" starts gnawing at me with a more personal dilemma: *"Do you really think you can live up to Weegee's expectations after that weekend? Come on….you're an average guy with average parts, and not a helluva lot of experience. Do you want to end up a one hit wonder or would you rather she remember you as 'White Lightnin'?"*

Ya' see what's happening here? In my mind, I'm already planting the seeds for failure, which will definitely happen, now that I'm worried about it. Shit!

Suddenly, taking a stand for what's right and what I feel takes a back seat to my little *"Man Voice"* telling me, *"Quit while you're ahead. Don't be a fucking loser!"*

Well, I punk out and never answer the letter, or the next two. My fragile ego remains intact, but my moral compass takes a big hit. So much for the idealistic, philosophic, seeker of truth. When push comes to shove, like most men, I think with my dick.

Chapter IV

Dispatches from Ghosts in My Head

Ghosts in Baseball Caps

I'm invisible to most of you,
except on Veteran's Day
and Memorial Day.
I'm that grey haired old guy,
in the funny ball cap,
with the gold writing,
and strange looking
insignias on the front.

If you choose to see me,
I might be sitting quietly,
on a bench in the mall,
waiting for my wife
to finish shopping,
or at the library
trying to figure out how
to work the damned computer,
or maybe,
I just pass you on the street.
You never notice me.

Sometimes I have a cane or a walker,
and sometimes
I'm riding one of those funny looking electric scooters
with a faded black and white
POW flag, flappin' on a pole,
fastened to my seat with duct tape.

We're the ghosts of wars past,
both Hot and Cold.
We see each other.
A smile and a nod,
signal brotherhood and pride

when we pass.

We make our way,
as best we're able,
bearing memories,
of past glories
and for some, past horrors.
The weight of these memories,
both good and bad,
are still carried with pride.

Canes, walkers, and scooters,
may be our current
means of transportation,
but do not signify
any weakening of spirit.

You wave flags
when we leave,
you cheer when we return,
and then,
go on with your lives,
leaving us invisible
'till the next parade,
when again, we're saluted;
For what?
To ease your guilt
for service not shared?

There's a large wall mural
in the lobby of
the Manhattan Veteran's Hospital.
It bears the words,
The Price of Freedom Is Evident Here
Twenty-two returned veterans

commit suicide every day.
On any given night,
more than 300,000 veterans are living on the streets.
You really want to do something?
Forget the salute.
Volunteer time or money to The Gary Sinise Foundation
or the Disabled American Veterans charity.
That's a meaningful tribute to those who've served.

Wounded Warrior

An Irish American boyo,
young and sweet,
from the Jersey shore,
quits the seminary and joins up
because.....
"It's the right thing to do!"

Idealism, innocence?
Lost forever,
somewhere in the rice paddies
in Southeast Asia
back in 1967.

We spat at the man
who came home.
We called him "murderer"
and "baby killer."
Yet, we sent him off to fight again,
on college campuses;
ordered him to fire on students with rubber bullets.
What were we thinking? *"Let's really fuck this guy up?"*

Now, he watches only movies made before 1960.
"Gave up on politics with LBJ!"
He hates politicians, hates "Hanoi Jane," religion, Hippies,
Punks, and especially war protesters.
He drinks way too much Bud Lite
and watches the Mets lose on TV,
unwilling and unable
to walk or even stand anymore...

"I'm no hero. I was just tryin' to save my own ass," he tells me.
A Bronze Star and Purple Heart claim otherwise.

Buried deep in his nightmares,
the truth hides, unreleasable,
as though confined to solitary.

His woman is the target
now of his anger,
and each bears the scars,
both mental and physical,
of their private war.

Housebound for years and likely to die there,
his hair goes uncut and mostly unwashed,
his nails untrimmed;
an eerie visage of an "end stage" Howard Hughes.

Cancer almost kills him....
Too angry to die that way,
Seemingly broken, yet unrepentant,
his statement to the world is Fuck you!
To most,
all they see
is a shell of a man,
but if you could hold him close to your ear,
you just might pick up a faint trace,
of ocean waves rolling in,
on the Jersey shore.

Riley

We buy a little bungalow in the Catskills in 1982,
during the Iran Hostage Crisis.
There are long lines at gas stations
and mortgage rates are 18%.
This area is so poor and run down
that its red lined by banks.
You can't get a mortgage there,
even if you're dumb enough
to want to pay the going rate.
The owner finances this beat up old place for 10%,
just so he can get out from under it.

My wife and I have zero credit,
and borrow the cheap down payment
from both our parents,
with the stipulation that we repay them within two years,
at market rate interest.
Nothing like family love, huh?

What sells us on this place
is the spectacular view from the front porch,
a mowed field across the road,
with a pond and a mountain view behind.
The sun comes up on the porch every morning
and makes the house glow.
But ... it's painted pink.

Inside, there's tacky flowered contact paper, for wallpaper.
The kitchen consists mostly of an $89,
imitation Formica, counter/cabinet combination,
from Rickles Discount store.
The bathroom walls are covered in oilcloth
and maroon imitation tiles made of plastic.

"I love you" is scrawled on the bedroom closet door, with lipstick,
and all of the baseboards and woodwork are painted pink.
It looks like some stoner hippie romantic lived here.

The place has been rented off and on
for over twenty-five years.
In the unfinished basement
we find a punching bag
and a setup to reload bullet casings.

We have no money,
so we spend the first year cleaning up mattress springs,
rusted old beer cans, and .38 caliber bullet casings from the lawn.
The place has gone unrented for the past several years.
It's a mess.

I spend a part of the second summer
putting two coats of light yellow paint with white trim,
over the fading pink outside.
My friend Sean, an artist from the city, is helping me,
and at days' end,
we sit on the porch drinkin' beer
and smoking a little weed.
We call our wives every night
just to tell them how magnificent the sunsets are.

We put in a flower bed
alongside the house by the kitchen door,
and dig up a small place off from the house,
to plant some Jersey tomatoes
from seeds my uncle gave us.

It ain't pretty, but we have our first home.
We're happy and we're in love.
My wife and I collect old junk furniture

and household goods
from the trash, our friends, and family
and decide that this will be our retirement home
down the road sometime.

I wake up one Saturday morning
to find a greasy piece of notepaper
taped to our kitchen screen door.
Scribbled on it is,
"Best stop stealing stone from my property wall, or *ELSE*."
Signed, "Your neighbor."

Well, if you know anything at all about Sullivan County,
you know that you can't dig an inch of dirt without hitting stone.
That's why most old properties are bordered by stone walls,
laid there when the ground was cleared.
My surveyor placed my property line markers
smack in the middle of the stone walls
surrounding our property,
so legally the stone wall belongs to both sides.
Having retrieved plenty of stone
from digging a flower garden and tomato patch,
I certainly have no good reason
to be stealing stones from anyone.
We're trying to figure out
where to dump the stones
we've already dug up.

I decide to pay a visit to our neighbor.
Since I've already learned that the locals don't much like city folks,
particularly Italians and Jews,
I pack my .22 magnum, two shot derringer in my back pocket,
cross over the stone wall,
and head up the hill looking for a house.

I hike past an overgrown apple orchard,
through acres of freshly timbered land,
until I reach a lake, brown with pine needles and beaver dams,
with a small very rustic shack by the side of it.

I slosh through deep mud up to the front of the shack
and knock on a crudely made wooden door several times
with no response.
Finally, the door slowly creaks open a few inches
and a voice growls, *"What?"*
I reply, "I'm your neighbor."
I slip the scribbled note from my door through the opening.
It's taken by an unseen hand. Silence.

After about two minutes,
the door swings partially open to reveal my new neighbor.
He's not so much old as worn out looking:
unshaven, wearing a stained V neck T-shirt and dirty overalls.
His hair is sparse, grey, and unwashed.
When he finally speaks, it's apparent most of his teeth are gone
 and he kind of blubbers his words out through sunken lips.
"Come in, boy."

The door opens and I step into a small dark cavern,
piled from floor to ceiling with newspapers and magazines,
with only a small winding path to walk through.
He leads me along the path of newspapers
into a second larger room that's sparsely furnished
with a sink, a small bed, a wood stove in the center,
and a curio cabinet filled with tiny figurines.
It is totally out of place in this dungeon.
There are two small chairs by the stove.
He gestures me to take a seat.

"Cup of tea?"

"Sure."

He walks to the small sink and picks up two china cups.
He pulls a dirty handkerchief from his back pocket
and carefully wipes them after running a bit of water on them.
He takes them to the stove
and pours two cups of tea from a cast iron kettle.
He hands me a cup and sits.
"Well?" he says.

I tell him, "I've got my own good supply of dug up stone,
so I certainly have no reason
to be stealing any from the wall.
And for your information,
my property line runs through the center of that stone wall,
so I'm legally half owner of those stones."

"What's your name, boy?"

"Phillip Giambri. Yours?"

"Riley," he says.
Silence.
*"Looks to me like some of them stones on my wall are missing.
Know anything about that if it's not you?"*

"Looks to me like that wall
has been falling apart for a long time,
and hasn't been mended or cared for by anyone.
Why be concerned now?
Is it because I moved in next door?"

Silence.
*"Just figured your kind come up from the city
and think everything's yours for the taking."*

81

"Well you best be doing some rethinking on that,
'cause the last thing I need is more stone."

We sit for a bit drinking our tea.
Finally, I stand and walk over to the curio cabinet
and look at the figurines.
He says, "Ever been to Japan?"

"No"

*"Well those are ancient Japanese Ivory miniatures.
Collected them for years when I was overseas."*

"And how did you come to be spending so much time "overseas?"

"Did some time with the Navy."

"Me too."

"Yeah, where?"

"Submarines. North Atlantic mostly.
Off the coast of Russia during the Cold War."

His demeanor suddenly softens
and he breaks into what could almost pass for a sly grin
through those caved in lips.

"What'd you do?" I asked.

"(MACV-SOG)"
Pause .....
"Military Assistance Command, Vietnam – Studies and Observations Group."

"What's the hell does that mean?"

"Joint Unconventional Warfare Task Force.
We did strategic reconnaissance, covert operations,
psychological warfare.... a little bit of a lot of shit."

"Really? When?"

"Early '60s."

"In Nam?"

"Mostly Laos and some others, before it all got big and bad."

He stands and says, *"I need some air."*

We make our way through the musty smelling newspaper tunnel
and out to the front of the shack.
He starts toward the lake
and I notice he kinda drags his right leg some.

"Arthritis got you?"

"Naah. Got in some shit up in the mountains with the Hmong.
We were tryin' to shut down the Ho Chi Minh Trail
and cut the supply line into Nam. Didn't go too well.
Took a round in the hip.
One of them Hmong threw his body over mine.
He took the rest of 'em.
Good soldiers, them Hmong."

Silence as we both stare off into the lake.

"So how's a guy like you,
who collects ancient Japanese ivory figurines,
and did Special Ops for the military,
end up in this shithole Sullivan County?"

"Don't much like bein' around people anymore,
and this is as good a place as any to be alone."
He asks, *"Do you hunt?"*

"No. I'm not much for eating meat
and don't see any point in killing for no good reason. *"*

"Well somebody's been up here
trophy hunting deer,
leaving bodies with no heads.
I catch 'em and there's gonna be some hell to pay.
This land's all posted
and I don't like trespassers
with no respect for wildlife on my land."

"Do you ever get lonely up here?"

"Nope"
Silence, then,
"I teach proper English
to those Spanish kids from the city
over at the Prison.
I bring some food to folks over the mountain
that're pretty needy.
You know there's a lot of really bad off folks up here
whose kids don't eat regular.
That bothers me some.
I try to help a little.
I get good money from the government."
He looks me in the eye.
"I'm thinkin' I've already run off my mouth too much
and it's best you be goin'."

"Well Riley, it's been nice meeting you
and I hope you see that I'm just looking to be a good neighbor."

"Eye-talian, that name?"

"What?"

"I'm askin' if you're Eye-talian."

"Italian American."

"Not too many around here.
Best watch your back with the Woodchucks."

"Woodchucks?"

"Yeah, the locals. They don't much take to your kind."

"What about you? Do they ever bother you?"

"Nope. They keep their distance.
They've learned better."

On that mysterious reply,
I shake his hand
and head off around the lake
back toward my house.
I call out, "See ya, Riley!"

"So long, kid!"

Over the next year,
there's a lot more good oak and maple
taken out of there by lumber haulers,
must be worth thousands.

Next I hear, he's sold off the place
to some rich family from Long Island.

I never see him again. Vanished!

After thirty years of hard work
making that bungalow into our dream home,
that plan to retire there eventually vanishes too,
like Riley.

Chapter V

Portraits

The Little Rock

I: <u>Prelude</u>

Her parents
must have had a premonition,
for of seven children,
they choose to name this child
Pietralina, after her grandmother.
It means Little Rock.

Antonio and Santa marry young
and sail steerage class
from the desolate poverty of Sicily
to
the Sanctuary Of The Hopeless,
America.

They struggle to make a life
as the Great Depression
slowly gnaws away
the meager remnants
of their American Dream.

Poverty and illness visit
and are warmed at their hearth.
Influenza, Measles, Tuberculosis,
Heart Attack, and Cancer;
each take their toll.
Pietralina, the Little Rock,
somehow survives,
The Great Depression.
By the nineteen fifties,
only three remain
of this luckless clan of nine:
Margaret, Angelina, and

Pietralina.
They bear the family children
but none, the family name.

Finally, there is just one.
Pietralina alone remains,
to walk the paths at Holy Cross,
honoring the graves of her kin.
She places a solitary flower
by each headstone,
offers a silent prayer,
and locks their memories
and their dreams in her heart.

II: <u>Building a Dream</u>

She appears to me always
as a wall
of warmth and strength,
solid and permanent,
like a rock.
Propelling her life forward
by sheer stubbornness and will,
she meets each adversity with
the power of faith and
the protection
of the Sicilian "red ribbon."
The *Malocchio* cannot penetrate
Pietralina, the "Little Rock."

She chooses to marry a boy
Tuberculosis has marked
for early death.
Against all objections,
they forge a new family and home

from the broken dreams
of both their lives.

Long sweatshop days,
followed by lonely,
trolley ride, hospital nights,
visiting first the husband,
then the son.
An eternity of bedside vigils.
She remains the "Little Rock."

Plowing through each adversity
like a demon train,
she determines not to be stopped
in pursuit of her family's dream:
Pinafore dresses, prom dreams,
Chevy Impala, mink stole,
lawn mower, catholic school,
diamond ring, air conditioner,
Miami winters, and children's graduations!
She remains steady
and labors tirelessly through it all.

III: <u>Approaching Darkness</u>

Overnight it seems, things change.
Suddenly, it's back to the city.
Gone is the house in the "burbs."
Gone next, the children,
and finally her faithful pet, Coco .
Pietralina, shudders a little
but doesn't know why.

The boy marked for death
survives everyone's prediction,

by more than 50 years.
She nurtures him, bewilders him,
cares for him, torments him,
and has enough love
for both of them.

She is his crutch,
and she is his cross to bear.
When he is gone,
a long silence remains.
A final whisper speaks
the unspeakable fear:
She is alone.

Ozzie and Harriet dreams,
of family arriving,
for a Walton Mountain Christmas,
turn to long days and nights alone.
Hurt, she feels the family door
has been slammed hard in her face.
Pietralina, feels the cold of night alone,
for the first time in her life.

She has no weapons
for the fight with "alone."
The rock weakens
and cries out for help
but family is "busy."
Storms of fear
seem to wash away her footing,
and a gradual slide begins for
Pietralina, the Little Rock.

When family fails her,
she is forced to confront

her demon alone.
She must fight for her life,

Through prayer,
she finds God is there,
waiting to embrace her,
and reveal her own truths:
She finds the strength
she's always provided
for others,
in their struggles.

IV: Rebirth

Time and prayer are her healers
and she is reborn.
The dormant volcano stirs again,
and lets flow a wall of fire,
with new will and new wonder.
She finds a new beginning,
a new life...this one, her life.

This poem is the song of her life,
and remains her only reward
for a lifetime
of selfless giving.
She triumphs over all,
by lending age
such beauty and grace.

I'm often chided
for being stubborn to a fault,
for grabbing on
and refusing to let go.
For me,
it's a badge of honor

that I wear with pride,
for it was passed on to me
by my mother
Pietralina, the "Little Rock."

Awkward Girl

At twelve
she sprouts up suddenly,
like a roadside weed:
a skinny, awkward, 5'8"
clumsy, pre-pubescent girl
who wears glasses and plays the cello.
That's about as nerdy as you can get.

She slinks along
hunched over at the shoulders,
head down,
eyes focused on her feet,
trying to look smaller, shorter, invisible;
trying to hide the newly emerging breasts
that seem to be always at eye level,
for the boys in her class
to gawk at and laugh.

But...
just two years later,
it's all changed.
Boys in her high school classes
are taller than her now,
and she's blossomed
into a beautiful, statuesque,
full busted, blonde bombshell,
who attracts boys
like bears to honey.

Still embarrassed a bit by her height,
she dates mostly basketball players,
and inadvertently
becomes one of the "in crowd"

94

and part of the high school elite.
No more the nerdy loser,
a new sense of confidence breeds a smile
that'll break the hearts,
of most of boys in her class.

Along with that great smile,
are those 34Ds,
causing a sensation,
whenever she shows up
at the town pool,
in her California bikini.

The blond hair and those boobs
are gonna' be her ticket
out of a blue collar world,
into the "Leave It To Beaver" TV show
middle class life she longs for.

That dream crashes and burns at eighteen, though.
Knocked up in her first year of college,
it's a shot-gun wedding,
followed months later
by a still-born baby girl.

The winning smile is gone now,
and the 34Ds?
They're gorged with milk
waiting for that little girl gone.

A marriage doomed from the start:
Seven years of depression
fighting memories
of a baby held hopelessly
for only a moment.

The road to middle class Utopia
vanishes before her eyes.
An impending divorce,
leaves her fleeing to New York City.
She reaches out to an old college roommate,
who offers shelter
and eventually,
a blind date with a friend.
When asked what he's like,
her friend replies,
"Hey, he likes blondes with big boobs.
You're perfect."

"I don't think I'm ready for this yet."

"Trust me on this one!"

In anticipation of this blind date,
the once confident high school "hottie,"
falters back to the awkward,
hunched over, twelve-year-old.

Prepared for the worst,
the blind date offers instead,
a humble, decent looking, blue collar guy.
There is an immediate and strong
mutual attraction on this first date,
and within days, they're inseparable.

The hunched over twelve-year-old
once again transforms
into the buxom blonde.
New found happiness
brings back that endearing smile,

and those 34Ds
are privately admired now
only by her lover.

Life takes on a new beginning
with revived hope
of living that middle class dream.
Happy years of travelling, working, sharing a life,
are meticulously documented by her
in countless photos,
hoping to preserve these good memories,
and the deep love they share.

By forty
those 34Ds are not quite as firm as they used to be.
She's starting to get a bit self-conscious about them again,
so now the bikini's retired
for a one-piece bathing suit.
She still looks amazing, and life is good,
so fuck it!
Mid-forties,
she detects a lump in her right breast.
It begins a perilous journey,
shared with doctors, surgeons, radiologists,
and that blue collar guy who loves her.

Within a year,
a second lump is discovered
in her left breast,
requiring more doctors, more surgery,
and briefly, a loss of hope.
That hunched over twelve-year-old
is back again,
trying to hide the destruction
going on in her chest.

Blue collar grit
make her a fighter though,
and she eventually regains
her strength and her life.
The surgeries leave those once proud 34Ds
a good bit smaller,
but hey, they're still there
and they're actually
a bit more firm, than they were at forty.
She passes the five-year mark,
and a "thumbs up" from her doctors,
offers a big sigh of relief.

After ten years,
the painful memories are mostly faded,
but the long thin scar on each breast
remains
as a reminder,
of how fine a line there was,
between life and death

That awkward twelve-year-old,
turned blonde bombshell,
matured into a strong, independent,
working professional,
happily married,
and a survivor...
my wife.

Ingrid's Story

Ingrid Washinawatok grew up on the Menominee Indian Reservation in Wisconsin. At birth she was given the Native American name, "Flying Eagle Woman." She became politically and socially active as a teenager in the '60s and joined the militant American Indian Movement, or AIM, the Indian equivalent of The Black Panther Party. They sent her to college in Cuba where she met and fell in love with Ali, a combat hardened "Freedom Fighter" from Lebanon. They married, moved to Brooklyn, and had a beautiful baby boy.

Ingrid devoted her life to helping indigenous women and children improve their lives and retain their ethnic culture. She traveled extensively on her mission for The Fund of the Four Directions, and in 1999, along with two other Americans, went to the jungles of Columbia to establish a school for native children that would help them retain their cultural roots. The three Americans were kidnapped by the FARC, a Right Wing paramilitary group that earned money escorting drug dealers and kidnapping tourists for ransom. Coincidentally, President Clinton donated $1 million dollars to the Columbian Government to fight drug traffickers, and in a rapid response, the FARC tortured and murdered the three American hostages. Their bodies were discovered a week later, across the border in Venezuela, in a farmer's field. All who knew her were devastated. She was the first Menominee woman ever to be honored with a full Warrior's death ceremony and burial. I offered this piece at her funeral on the reservation:

Smoke Dancers

The earth journey ends
in a farmer's open field,
their passage marked only
by a salute of gunfire.

Like signal smoke,
the spirits
rise from the field
to dance on the wind,
embracing and comforting
ten thousand hearts
broken
by the bullets.

A Seamstress Story

March 25th marks the anniversary of the Triangle Shirtwaist Factory fire. It was the deadliest industrial disaster in the history of New York City, resulting in the deaths of 146 garment workers. They died from fire, smoke inhalation, or falling to their deaths because fire truck ladders only reached the fifth floor. Most of them were Jewish and Italian immigrant women aged sixteen to twenty-three; the oldest was 48, and the youngest was 11.

The managers locked the doors to the stairwells and exits to prevent pilferage and unauthorized breaks. Many of the workers jumped from the eighth, ninth, and tenth floors. That fire led to legislation requiring improved factory safety standards and helped spur the growth of The Ladies' Garment Workers' Union, which fought for better working conditions for sweatshop workers. That factory was located downtown in New York City on Washington Place.

Associated Press - November 25, 2012
DHAKA, Bangladesh
112 people were killed in a fire that raced through a multi-story garment factory outside Bangladesh.

Associated Press – May 13, 2013 - SAVAR, Bangladesh
Following the collapse of a Bangladesh garment factory building the death toll has reached 1,127, making it the worst disaster in the history of the global garment industry.

****

During the Great Depression,
my mom had to quit school at seventeen
to work as a seamstress in a sweatshop.
She eventually worked her way up
to a job in a union clothing factory
thanks mostly, to the Japanese bombing Pearl Harbor.

Looking back at the terrible working conditions,
it seems now that the only difference

101

between a clothing factory and a sweatshop
was that one was a legal business with "union representation" and the other wasn't.
Conditions were appalling in both environments,
although, agreeably worse in sweatshops.
To me it was just mom's job and seemed perfectly normal.

The Amalgamated Garment Workers Union
valued only tailors as union members,
and they were exclusively men.
Women were relegated to machine work
for the length of their "careers."
Union Shop Stewards told members
who they were to vote for in all elections,
from union locals, up to presidential races.
They watched you when you voted in the shop,
and you voted the union ticket,
or suffered the consequences.
Mom, like most women, went along with the program,
kept her head down, and pushed pants through the machine. Violence was common
during elections in the shops
but was relegated mostly to the men.
Women kept their mouths shut and their heads down.

A young man could start as a "bundle boy"
carrying bundles of clothing to the female machine operators.
If he was sharp and/or had "connections"
he could become an apprentice tailor in a few years,
and if he was stamped "okay" by the union and the other tailors,
his career was made.
Women had only two options;
push clothes through the machines
until they either quit or died.

Sewing machine operators are paid "piece work,"
that is,

they are paid for each piece of clothing
they complete their portion of the job on.
Mistakes are costly because they have to be corrected
and that cuts production time for the day.

During World War II,
mom worked at the Philadelphia Quartermaster's Depot
sewing linings in heavy wool army coats.
Dad picked her up after work every day
in the cab he was driving,
and they loaded her "mistakes" in the cab.
We spent family evenings unstitching her mistakes
so mom would lose less time at work.

She learned quick and worked hard.
Over the years she changed jobs often
and progressed up to a coveted position as a Braid Stitcher.
Braid Stitchers sew the shiny satin stripes
on the side of men's tuxedo pants.
Its a four part operation (sewing two sides of two braids)
and considered one of the better positions in the factories,
because it pays a higher piece rate than most other jobs.

Mom became highly skilled, very fast,
and gained a reputation in the industry.
She was known everywhere as "Bea the Braid Stitcher."
and was sought after by all tuxedo manufacturers.
Mom was a workhorse and she flourished.
Other factory owners were always trying to "draft" mom,
to work for them.
She commanded the highest rates,
and if she really busted ass,
she could make a sustenance living,
but she still needed a second income for us to survive,
so on her lunch breaks,

she sold chocolates to the other workers.

Arthritis eventually crippled mom's fingers
and she had to quit working when she was fifty-five.
She never collected a penny in benefits
because the union contract
required that you work until sixty-two
to be eligible for a pension and health benefits,
no matter how many years you had worked.
Thirty-eight years of indentured servitude,
and she was left with no union benefits whatsoever.

Fuck you Amalgamated Garment Workers Union!
Your alligator skin shoes and those sharkskin suits
came at the cost of my mom's arthritic fingers,
and the millions of other union women,
whose lungs where choked with clothing dust,
while you sucked the life blood from them, and prospered.
Unions helped create the middle class in America,
yet you became,
the same as the monsters
you were supposed to protect them from.

Those jobs all go overseas now
and the workers there are subjected
to the same horrible working conditions
that spurred the birth of the union movement here.

Our greedy American companies
buy from whoever makes the cheapest garments
and these workers average about $.20 an hour.
And some of our friendly union goons
continue to make money,
by selling Union Labels to factory owners
who have them sewn in their imported garments

so we all think we're "buying American."
"Look for the Union Label?"
I'm lookin' for some Karma payback here!

Chapter VI

Notes to My Shrink
(If I Ever Get One)

This Face

No matter who I think I am,
no matter who I pretend to be,
no matter who I fantasize I am,
no matter who I now think
I would like to be,
the truth lies apparent:

This life I've chosen,
this life I've lived,
the sins I've committed,
whatever good I've done,
the friends I've I faulted,
the friends I've lifted,
the family I've betrayed,
the family I've honored,
the honesty I've offered,
the lies I've told,

the asses I've kissed,
the enemies I've fought,
the lives I've blessed,
the promises I've broken,
the ideals I've upheld,
the values I abandoned,
the principals I've lived by,
bravery shown when least expected,
silence when protest was required,
the gods I've prayed to,
and the gods I've cursed,
the stumbles and falters,

The good and the evils,
are all illuminated
in the worn out vestige

107

of this façade
of youthful idealism,
that remains,
but lies hidden in shame,
for the me that never was,
the me I could have been,
the me I should have been.

I have but one remaining enemy
who challenges me daily
to be the me who is better
than the me I am;
My enemy,
the face in the mirror.

These scars, wrinkles,
and lines, bear testament
to the truth of who I've been,
and who I am now.

Each morning
a face is revealed
that is the sum of my life.
I wear this face I've earned.
It's the face I deserve.

Only Skin Deep

Sometimes you meet someone
for the first time,
and you immediately
form an impression,
of who you think they are,
based almost entirely
on what they look like.

You're thinkin' to yourself,
"Geez, that poor bastard's really ugly."
or, *"She'll never get a husband with that face."*
or *"Goddamn, she's hot, I gotta' hit on that one."*
or *"Damn he's good lookin',*
I bet he gets more ass than a toilet seat."
or something like that.
It's embarrassing to admit,
but I think a lot of us are guilty
of these kinds of instant judgments.

Something strange often happens
when I'm put in a situation where
I get to know a lot more about the person,
either as a friend or coworker.
Over a period of time,
they seem to slowly transmogrify,
into first, a more "normal" looking person,
then eventually,
into someone whose looks
I don't even notice or consider anymore.

The opposite is also sometimes true.
I've been closely involved with people
considered very physically beautiful or attractive,
yet as I get to know more about them,

they become less and less attractive to me,
until it actually seems,
that they've become physically ugly,
largely because on what I've perceived
as "character flaws"
or disingenuous on their part.
One day, they're just ugly!

I guess once you peel off the skin layer,
all that's left is "the truth,"
and that's what sometimes causes
the seemingly dramatic change
in their physical appearance.

So, in conclusion,
all I can say is,
that if you spend enough time around me,
I just might grow on you,
or not!

Remembrance of 9/11

Resurrecting 9/11 memories for me, is like ripping out shards of broken glass protruding through that horrible white dust cloud.

In the mid-70s, my wife and I get reservations at Windows of The World, "the must-go-to" restaurant of the moment. We leave carrying a tourist brochure with a header reading, *"The closest some of us will ever get to heaven."* Seems kind of ominously prophetic now.

September 11, 2001 I report for jury duty at the Courthouse near City Hall. I arrive a bit early and sit in the park across from the courthouse with a coffee, enjoying the beautiful fall morning. I'm blinded by the morning sun bouncing off the face of the twin towers and slip on my Ray Ban aviators. The air is clean, I'm feelin' good, and it's one of those New York moments.

I report in and just get seated, when I hear and feel a muffled rumbling of some kind. I assume it's a subway underneath the courthouse pulling through the station. One of the jurors is listening to a small radio with an ear bud attached. He announces that a plane crashed into the World Trade Center (WTC).

Wow. We can't actually see the WTC from the courtroom but we're soon overwhelmed with the sounds of sirens speeding by all around us. It seems like moments later, that the juror announces a second plane hit the other tower. Suddenly, the doors of the courtroom burst open, and men are shouting, "FBI… you have to leave immediately." The FBI building is adjacent to the courthouse and these guys quickly take charge of evacuating the courthouse and surrounding buildings. Everyone is hustled out of the buildings and herded east, away from the towers. Once outside, we all stare up at the towers to see what's going on. It seems unreal. My first thought is to go home, grab my camera, and come back to take pictures of the evacuations and rescues.

Police quickly channel thousands of evacuees and keep us moving swiftly uptown, via the Bowery. Countless people are safely evacuated very quickly; an amazing accomplishment, considering what is about to happen.

My fellow juror with the radio walks ahead of me. I try to keep up so I'll hear any new developments. He suddenly shouts out, "The Pentagon was just bombed and it's on fire." Now that scares the shit out of me. This means we're at war now. But with who? The crowds walk briskly in silence, like a huge marching army, but constantly sneaking glances back at the burning Towers.

Back in my apartment I'm digging around for my camera, and turn on the TV just as the first tower collapses. I can't believe what I'm seeing. I freeze and just stand there watching the dust cloud thunder toward the terrified people running right at the TV cameras. I won't be going back there today.

The phone rings and jars me back to reality. My wife's friend tells me that my wife is being evacuated from Rockefeller Center where she works, and is worried because she knows I'm downtown. She asks her to check on me. "I'm okay... I think!"

Our neighborhood is in chaos. Heavy smoke, dust, and sirens everywhere. I close the windows, put on the air conditioner, and sit by the TV, trying to comprehend what's happening. It just keeps getting worse with each passing minute. My wife arrives safely by mid-afternoon. We both continue to stare at the TV in disbelief.

As a hospital employee, I need to get to work as soon as possible, but the streets are cordoned off, transportation shut down, and cars aren't being allowed to pass. My boss calls and says he'll pick me up if I can get to 14th street, and be sure to have my hospital ID with me. I walk up First Avenue to 14th to find it lined with armed military and police in full combat gear, weapons loaded, and armored vehicles everywhere. When I explain that I work at a hospital and show my ID, they allow me to pass on to 15th street where my boss is waiting. We encounter checkpoints all the way to 70th and York, and arrive to find our Trauma Team is being dispatched to Ground Zero, to assist with casualties. Most of the staff volunteer to stay as long as necessary, to assist in any way possible, including blood donations. My crew all sleep in the auditorium in scrubs, wrapped in blankets.

No victims or casualties ever arrive, and when that reality sinks in, a dark silence settles over everyone, as I'm sure it did in every other hospital in the city. No one to help, no one to save, no one rescued, no one alive. The depth of the horror begins to sink in.

As days and weeks go by, we all slowly work ourselves back into our daily routines, but normal will never be normal again. My wife returns to her office at Rockefeller Center overlooking St. Patrick's Cathedral. She bears witness to a seemingly endless dirge of kilted drummers and pipers, fire trucks draped in funeral bunting and flags, and a sea of blue uniforms lining 5th Avenue, offering a final salute to lost brothers and sisters.

New Yorkers will bear a scar from a wound so deep in the heart that it will never completely heal. We watch on TV as our president declares war to avenge the killings. I guess it's supposed to make us feel better. It doesn't.

I'm Waiting

I've reached that age now
where,
when I go to bed at night,
I'm thankful
for having made it through another day.

Yet, every morning,
I wonder if today
is gonna' be "*that*" day.
You know:
"*that*" day,
when something doesn't seem quite right
with the old bod
and you wait a few hours
to see if things are gonna get better.
They don't.

So I wait patiently on hold
for an appointment
with my doctor.

Then I'm in the waiting room,
hoping to see the doctor.

Now I'm in the exam room,
undressed,
in an open backed gown,
on a metal table,
waiting for the doctor.
It's cold.
Then I'm waiting for some blood work,
and I'm waiting for some x-ray results.

Now I'm waiting for a clear diagnosis.

114

and I'm waiting to hear what my chances are
for a complete recovery.

I wait to begin treatment,
then I'm waiting for treatment to end.
I'm waiting for rehab,
and then waiting for rehab to end.

Now I'm waiting for my doctor to say
I'm good as new.
But he doesn't,
and he won't.

So now I'm waiting
for that knock on the door.
It's The Grimm Reaper.
He says, "I've been waiting for you!"

I Don't Believe in Heaven

I don't believe in heaven,
but if I try to imagine
what a heaven *could* be like for me,
it would be an eternal video loop
of all of those moments in my life
that I've experienced, and seen, and felt,
and thought: "Man ...... I wish this would last forever."

It's sitting in my dad's lap,
hands on the steering wheel
of our '39 Plymouth,
driving down a country dirt road.
He lets me think
that I'm driving the car.
Wow!

I'm eight years old,
lying alone on a bed of moss and leaves
on the forest floor,
with the sound of water rolling over stones,
and a lone blue jay cawing
with an eerie echo that bounces off tree trunks
and rings in my ears;
with filtered beams of sunlight warming my body
as I lay, arms outstretched, staring up and smiling,
and I become one with the forest,
and experience a moment of pure ecstasy,
that I will never know again.
It's that intense burning in my chest
that I feel with my first schoolboy crush,
when the girl I secretly like,
leaves a valentine card on my school desk.

It would be that moment
lying on the hot sand beach
on the South Jersey shore
wet and smelling of ocean,
staring up at the sun,
through black frame Roy Orbison sunglasses,
after an afternoon of surf riding,
wanting my fifteenth summer to last forever.

Its riding a '48 Harley at full throttle
down US1 in Virginia
with thirty five cents in my pocket,
two bald tires, no helmet,
greased hair flying in the wind,
the speedometer pegged at 120,
and I know for sure
that at sixteen,
I am invincible.

It's that amazing Christmas Eve party
with my fellow acting school students
when we dance and drink, and yearn for sex,
and know for sure that we have talent,
and are gifted,
and will all soon be famous.

It's the first time I smoke pot
and play "Strip Tac Toe"
with beautiful female dancer friends,
and call my best buddy to tell him
that I've died and gone to heaven.

It's the exquisite moment
that my new wife and I first climax together
and know that we are now joined forever.

It's snowmobiling through a pine forest at night
with the headlight revealing a wonderland
of snow laden branches
glimmering like ghosts in the night.
Emerging from the woods
to speed across the frozen lake under a full moon.

It's riding Bucky at a full gallop
down the side of a mountain
in a furious rain storm,
singing "Riders In The Rain" at the top of my lungs,
while lightening's flashing insanely through the sky
all around us.

It has to include those stunning
Autumn weekends at my cabin
when the writing juices are flowing,
the mountains are ablaze with color,
and I want the beauty of the view
from my kitchen window
to remain in my eyes forever.

It would be watching the sun rising slowly
on a glazed frozen lake,
ice fishing at 10 below zero,
watching our "tip-ups" and sipping brandy.

It would be each moment
I'm about to finish a book that I love
and don't ever want to turn that last page.

"to dance beneath the diamond sky

with one hand waving free,
silhouetted by the sea."
That's Bob Dylan.

For me now,
it's hangin' at Earle's Hideaway
on the beach
with my veteran brothers
drinking, dancing,
and listening to good blues music
at two in the afternoon
with the sun beating down hard,
the music loud as hell,
and the working stiffs
all wishing they were us.
Fuck 'em all!
This is as close to heaven as I'll ever get.

Reflections 1967

How much of the man is himself
and how much is owned by the past?

I feel the roots of my family tree
nourishing and sustaining life in me.

I am but a small bud on a branch of this ancient tree
but without the flowering of my buds there will be no seed
and the tree will eventually wither and die.

I see in myself all who have given me life:
Giambri, Magazzu, Zagone, Munafo',
Baratta, Badame, Innoranti, Pagoria, and Patti;
names that seem to me exotic, romantic,
and both hard and brittle,
with many colors and textures.

All in their time contributed to the life and size of our tree.
Their blood flows through my veins
and their images are alive in my mind.
They direct me toward a destiny
that is more than mine alone.

The hot lazy sun of Sicily burns within me
yet my fingers lack the feel of the fertile soil
that was their sustenance
and life for hundreds of years.

My complexion is that of the city-bred
and sallow man of the subways.
My heritage demands that I fight to the death
for any affront to my name, my family's honor,
or the ideals that we bear in our blood.
The pride may be stung,
the adrenaline flows,
but my sword remains sheathed.

I find instead that I am part of a "metropolis,"

an indistinguishable mass
that daily gets shoved, cursed, defiled, and castrated
by other indistinguishable parts of the mass.
The enemy remains vague, anonymous, and elusive
like a terrorist in the night.

Therein lies the plight
of the second generation American:
Our ancestors fought, worked, and died
that we might know a better life than they.

If they could see for a moment through our eyes. . . .
We, the fruit of their proud trees,
work our days in tiny cells
hidden from sunlight, emerging at dusk
to breathe, not the crystal air of nature,
but a man made, man destroying concoction
of smog, industrial fumes, cigarette smoke,
and artificial pre-conditioned air.
Our lives are spent as logs
tossed onto the all-consuming fires
of "American development."

A part of me burns in that fire,
but another still feels the burn
of the hot Sicilian sun.
I stand with one leg on each continent,
not able to feel at home in either,
awaiting my destiny.

The bud has yet to flower
or bear seed.

What the Hell is Love?

I'm six years old,
and I know one thing for sure,
I love my mother.

At eight,
I really love my dog Penny.

At twelve,
I think I love Jesus.

At fourteen
I love Maureen,
but she likes my best friend.

At sixteen
I'm in love with Cass,
but I'm dating her best friend.

At eighteen I'm just angry.
I think no one loves me.
and I hate everyone.

At twenty-one,
Rosie really loves me,
but for almost a year,
I'm too drunk to notice
that she's a hooker,
and too drunk to care,
'cause I never really loved her.

At twenty-three
I'm madly in love with Carol;
we're even engaged,

until she dumps me
at twenty-five,
when I confess
I really want to be an actor
and not
the middle class banker,
I promised her.
I'm being selfish,
but still I'm heartbroken.

At twenty-six
Sharon and I are deeply in love,
but she tortures me
with flirtations
and endless tests
to prove that I love her.
After three years
of fights, anxiety, and exhaustion,
I just quit loving her.
It's then she chooses
to be the woman
I originally fell in love with,
but it's too late.
It's over.
She asks if we can at least
be "fuck buddies."
I say, "Sure, okay!"

At thirty
I'm in love with Eileen,
but
it's the onset of Women's Lib
and she weighs our relationship
in terms of what

her Woman's Support Group
feels is appropriate.
She dumps me
because they tell her,
I'm too "sexist"
and not
a "sensitive" enough guy.
She leaves a parting message
on my answering machine saying,
"Thanks. You helped me grow."
Grow what? A dick?
How's that for sensitive?

At thirty-two
I'm living with Susan.
She's a free spirit
and feels
an open sexual relationship
is necessary to fulfill herself
as a "woman."
She runs off to Canada
to live in a tee-pee,
with some hippie,
and leaves her needy sister behind,
until I work up the courage to kick her out.

I sleep with a lot of women
during these summers of
"Free Love"
but don't have much fun.
I get "The Clap" three times.

A friend offers a telling observation: "Ya know,
all the women

you fall in love with
are really the same fucked up person,
they just look different."

Wow!
A moment of clarity?
She offers a blind date
with her best friend
to prove her point.
I accept,
and believe I feel real love
for the very first time.

But, she's gone now
and almost 45 years later,
I find myself still wondering,
"What the hell is love?"
and realize
that I may never know.
The feeling now seems
more an abstraction
than a tangible sensation.

At this late stage of life,
I feel I know
as little about love
as when I started.
I'm very grateful
for the love I've been given,
but have no clear feeling,
for how much,
I've ever honestly returned.

The Soundtrack of My Life

I've been very blessed.
For as long as I can remember,
my life has been accompanied by music.
Moments and memories
are recorded and then replayed in my head,
whenever a song connects
to a memory.

My parents are part of The Great Generation.
They listen and dance to the sound of The Big Bands.
My childhood is filled with the music of the '40s,
and I know the words to every pop song,
before I start school.

My mom is a Bobbysoxer and a proud member
of the Russ Columbo and Frank Sinatra fan clubs.
Their framed pictures hang on our living room wall,
attesting to their stature as virtual family members.

When I'm six,
my parents buy me a Frank Sinatra sport jacket,
chocolate and tan with wide lapels,
just like the one Frank is wearing
in the picture in our living room.
I love it, and I love Frank Sinatra.

When Russ Columbo dies in a plane crash,
my mom mourns in true Italian fashion,
as though we've lost a relative.

That innocent generation of pop music fans,
unwittingly gives birth to a new generation of music fanatics:
Greasers & Rockers.

126

At thirteen, I listen to the only black radio station in Philly: WPLJ.
Jocko Henderson is the DJ and he's badass.
I hear "Work with Me Annie" for the first time,
listen to that dirty sax screeching and wailing,
and my body wants to move.
I want more.

The back-beat of the song "Sha-Boom"
gets stuck in my head.
I beg my mom for $.75.
I go to Nipper's Record Store
and buy my first 45 record.

I listen R&B and want to know more.
At the main library in Philly,
I become a student of the blues.
They have recordings from the Library of Congress.
Listening on a primitive set of headphones,
I discover Leadbelly, Blind Lemon Jefferson,
Louis Armstrong, Bessie Smith, Chicago Blues,
Barrel House piano, Ragtime, and Jazz.

But I want it all.
I find Native American drum music,
Tuva Throat Singers from Asia,
Olatunji's African Drums of Passion,
Cajun Zydeco,
Rural Appalachian Folk Music,
every kind of original indigenous music.
As long as I feel the beat, I'm addicted.
I can't get enough.

R&B gives birth to Rock & Roll.
and I know immediately that this is *my* music.

I can't afford to buy records
so I go to the local soda shop
on days when the guy puts the new records in the jukebox.
I beg him to sell me the old used ones.
He sees the hungry look in my eyes,
and sells them to me for $.25 cents each.
A young addict connects with his first dealer.

After school,
while my parents are still working,
I take long swigs of Seagram's 7
and dance alone in the basement
to the beat of the music.
Little Richard and Jerry Lee Lewis
are my dance partners.

At fourteen,
I'm going to YMCA dances
to watch the dance contests.
"Hell, I can do that shit."

I study the dancers until I find a girl
that I think really feels the music and the beat the way I do.
I work up the courage
to ask her to be my partner in a dance contest.
She agrees.
We click, and easily win the first dance contest we enter.

I soon realize,
that with the right music,
mostly Little Richard or Jerry Lee,
and the right partner,
I can't lose.
My mind and my body enter
a kind of altered state when I'm dancing,

as though watching myself from above.
It's not me dancing:
it's the music and the beat, that's taken over my body,
like some mystical religious experience.
I'm in a state of ecstasy when I'm dancing
and it's as addictive as any drug could ever be.
I'm inexhaustible and unbeatable.
I never lose a contest.

In the mid-sixties,
I'm still collecting R&B, Rock & Roll, and Blues music,
and I discover British rockers,
who, like me, have been immersed in American blues music;
The Rolling Stones, The Animals, Clapton, Van Morrison,
and other Brits.

I'm still dancing, but not in contests any more.
I'm in New York City now, so it's endless SoHo loft parties,
with hopes of free booze and getting laid;
and it works for me, for a long time.
And everywhere .... there's always the music,
synced with my life and locked in my memories forever.

The Rolling Stones, James Brown, Neil Young, Tom Waits,
Marvin Gaye, The Temptations, The Four Seasons, Aretha Franklin,
Janis Joplin, Kris Kristofferson, Martha Reeves, The Four Tops,
and on and on it goes.

In the '80s, Disco Fever breaks out in New York City.
I don't like the beat, or the sound; it's too plastic for me.
I abandon pop music
for the sound of Outlaw Country Music,
whose writer/performers,
have absorbed the classic Grand Old Opry sound,
added electric, and a heavy back beat,

and moved from The Opry
to the back rooms of dive bars,
where they're embraced by a new generation of rockers.
Waylon Jennings, Willie Nelson, Johnny Paycheck,
Hank Williams Jr., David Allen Coe, and Johnny Cash.
I feel the beat and love the lyrics.
They sing of freedom
and life outside the world of suits.

But Country goes glitter and Vegas.
It's back to the roots of rock again,
and I'm lovin' the hard beat and sound
of the Punk and Indie bands popping up
all over the East Village.

The rhythm, the beat,
and sound of all these influences
echo endlessly through my head,
connecting to images from my life.
My body still responds
when I hear and feel the beat of the music.
The music is in me, and is the soundtrack of my life.

About The Author

Phillip Giambri
"The Ancient Mariner"

A product of the streets of South Philadelphia, he obtained his deviant perspective on life listening to Jean Shepherd on WOR radio back in the '50s. Fleeing Philly at seventeen, he served in the US Navy Submarine Force, has been an actor, hairstylist, stoner, janitor, writer, drifter, recording engineer, hired hand, poet, traveling salesman, barfly, banker, biker, bronco buster, announcer, mail-order minister, photographer, and computer guru. He arrived in New York City in '68, joined the Hippie pilgrimage to St. Marks Place, and never left.

He's attended too many schools to mention, studying nearly everything, without ever attaining a degree in anything. His work has appeared in Artists in the Kitchen, "Walt's Corner" in The Long Islander, Silver Birch Press, and NewYorkCityTalking.com. He curates a popular monthly spoken word/poetry event, Rimes of The Ancient Mariner as well as special collaborative events with other artist/performers; most recently the very successful, Barflies & Broken Angels, The Losers Club, and What The Hell Is Love? He performs original solo shows as "The Barfly," "The Village Idiot," and "The Drunken Sailor." His website offers bored web surfers a glimpse into his futile search for self-discovery and meaning. He can be found regularly spinning yarns and telling tall tales anywhere that will tolerate him.

www.AncientMarinerTales.com

Photo by Mike Geffner

Gratitude

To Curly for forty-two years of unconditional love.

To Jean Shepherd who taught me how listening to stories on a radio, in the dark late of night, could stir imagination and create a make- believe world with words that I would embrace and strive to emulate.

To my mentor and personal hero,
Don Ulmer.

To the lovely Muse who taught me to believe in possibilities again,
Susan Tierney.

To Artist Linda Wulkan for painting my words into rainbows.

To my bar buddies who nourish me with endless love and stories:
Daffy Burke
Lawrence Carter
Edgar Degas
Shane Keogh
Maria Owens
Marvelous Marvin Mendlinger
Mike John Merlino
Jeremy Stratton
Chloe Sweeny
Christopher Townley
Remco van Vliet
Pants Wathern

To my fellow writer friends whose help, inspiration, and belief in me, gave me the courage to jump this cliff:
Nichole Acosta
Russell Atwood
Alessandra Francesca

Kofi Forson
Pauline Findlay
Elizabeth Gauthier
Mike Geffner
Aimee Herman
Blair Hopkins
Linda Kleinbub
Jane LeCroy
Donnie Lamon
Anthony Murphy
Tommy Pryor
Vincent Quatroche
Janet Restino
Marie Sabatino
Moira T. Smith
Mickey Wyte

To all my Rimes family brothers and sisters who proudly wear the
"Silver Tongued Devil" T-shirt

To my chosen family whose love and care keeps the darkness away,
Alexa Aviles and Frankie Correa
Kristen and John Lopos
Leandro Ramos and Bobby Stack

To my brothers in the U.S. Navy Submarine Force who've always had my back, will be the first to prick a prideful balloon, and who will laugh at me, with me, and about me at any opportunity. They have been the source, pride, and inspiration for much of the man I've become.

Brotherhood of the Phin

"Phil Giambri's style is rugged streetwise New York, smoothed by a lifetime of Jack Daniel's. The voice of a man who has lived a life worth telling about." - Mickey Wyte, author of the Amazon bestselling novel, "A Fashion to Kill."

"They say good stories happen to those who can tell them. The magic in Giambri's poetic voice comes from his ability to render our most closely-held human experiences into laughable, relatable anecdotes. He manages to be both journalistically dissociative and evocative in his honesty." – Blair Hopkins, Photojournalist, writer

"...like a shot of literary poteen poured down your throat - these pieces are unyielding, unforgiving, and finish strong." - Ryan McCurdy, musician, actor, writer, storyteller.

"Phillip Giambri is a writer of true merit and distinction. He creates poems and tales using the simplest ingredients: down-to-earth descriptions and dialog, salty humor and wry insights into human nature. Phillip has a generous soul and a thoughtful spirit. He's a guy with whom you'd be glad to share good times and bad times. Start reading his writing, and by the time you get to the bottom of the first page, you'll know you've made a lifelong friend." - Michael Lydon, musician, songwriter, and author "The Rolling Stones Discover America" and "Ray Charles: Man and Music."

"Phillip Giambri is a natural-born story-teller and a licensed detective of the heart. His narratives are peopled more often than not by the grizzled denizens of an urban underbelly, and these characters spring to life through the all-seeing eye of a streetwise raconteur who's set his sights on exposing the foibles of the human animal. The world he evokes is delivered to us through the lens of a master spy-- one gifted with both a keen sensitivity to the internal emotional realm and a subtle awareness of the details of the concrete world around him. These, in fact, are just the sort of refined and nuanced observational skills required to effectively convey a tale, and when combined with his willingness to lay his cards on the table in the interest of honest self-reflection the reader is taken on a moving, thought provoking and entertaining ride. You won't be bored. And ya might just learn something in the process." - Moira T. Smith, Poet

"Phillip (The Ancient Mariner) Giambri is a magician of sentiment. His stories are transformative time capsules that put you in the shoes of a submarining barfly with an affinity for keen observation. From the dank dive bar deviance of yesteryear to the quiet reflectiveness of a true American hero, Giambri's stories have their finger on the pulse of humanity. Love, death, race, politics, and the pursuit of truthfulness all tangled, twisted and tasty in the form of a collection of short stories that are teeming with heartwarming sentimentality." - Graham Willner, author, poet, spoken word artist.

"Phillip Giambri is a romantic, cruiser and bruiser. These tales possess power and spirit of an experienced man. He tells the truth so hard it hurts; a brutal honesty which captivates the mind and soul. Ever wanted a voice inside your head while sitting at a bar...? This is Phillip Giambri at his best, crushing the psyche with hard tales about dead beats, "the damned," romantic lost souls. A reader for the pissed on and beaten down or those who want an excuse to man-up, rebel, or cop an attitude of a Hollywood wino." - Kofi Forson, Blogger @ Black Cocteau

"Phillip Giambri is a two-headed fire-breathing dragon, and his first collection of poems and stories mercilessly and mercifully scorch the earth with hope and regret, anger and love, foolishness and cut-out-the-fucking-bullshit-ness, and get real, asshole. They are cynically sentimental, leaving the reader feeling at once hollow and powerless, then fully indestructible. This slim volume goes around world; sometimes in a hot-wired car speeding down a back country road, sometimes in a submarine deep in the Baltic Sea. But whether in a crowded Lower Eastside Dive Bar in the 80s or a Scottish Cemetery at the height of the Cold War, Giambri's lean and lusty prose brings both his ordinary and unique experiences to vibrant life." - Russell Atwood, Author "Losers Live Longer."

"What do you call a man of many talents, flaws and skills? This story telling Barfly put serious pen to paper and began to record the stories of his life. The open mic Barfly spawned The Ancient Mariner. His love of words are his passions. He has evolved into a Lower East Side (the pre gentrification model) celeb of no small repute. His recollections and observations bring tears to eyes and smiles to faces and, remarkably, often at the same time. I have to describe this enigmatic force of nature as beloved friend. Listen and you'll find yourself using those same words." Ron Gliates, Writer, Emcee, Comedian, Person of Interest.

"Phillip Giambri has the heart of a new born whose wounds are open under the crimson sun. It's the fierceness of a lion's roar to the beauty of a new lily blossoming in the dewy quiet forest, only to stumble upon a golden box hidden beneath the gritty dirt. Mr. Giambri's truth of life stories and poems illuminate with an incandescent warmth that reminds us to stand a little taller, laugh a little louder, and shed tears in our stale beer. For memory is archive to our lives as sand is to the hour glass, and in fleeting moments we relive them with him. His words permeate through the ether and even the trees know his name." Pauline Findlay- author of Mirror Images, poet.

"For Phillip, an East Village writer; I'm picturing lookin' down a long bar at Waits, Burroughs, Bukowski, Thompson, all on their feet, leanin', hunched over, all of 'em half a score shots or more into the early a.m., nighthawks like in a Hopper painting, only it's not a diner, it's a dive. Did I mention Dorothy Parker, danglin' her feet from her perch on a barstool, slummin', holdin' her own? And down at the far end, nursin' his well whiskey, takin' it all in, Phillip, only half-reactin' to Dorothy's dangerous come-ons, and the others bemused, askin' themselves, who's this tattooed submariner? Hey fellas, jus' a fellow raconteur, a chronicler of those dark late-night places frequented by boozers an writers with no better place to be." Gordon Gilbert, a West Village writer (takes one to know one).

"Phillip Giambri aka "The Ancient Mariner" is a preeminent storyteller whose tales are salty, sassy and nostalgic in one. He's a barfly who often meets damaged souls and sultry "crazy-eyed" ladies in his outings. He's not only drawn to Philly bebop music and the lure of cheap booze, but also to his late mother's work as a seamstress, a grueling job she carried out with pride and honor. Phillip's new book will take readers on many journeys, from sojourns around the world with old military pals, to East Village dive bars where he paints exquisite portraits of friends and neighbors with just the right dose of humor." Amy Barone, Poet and Author of Kamikaze Dance

"I met Phillip Giambri at a reading five years ago. We have since shared stories, shared a stage, shared a heritage, shared a cab, and shared a stuffed artichoke. He even shared his deceased wife's long, flowing dresses with me; the kind you see in a Fred Astaire/Ginger Rogers film, the ones that swirl and bounce and twirl with every step, and that's sort of how it is with his words, they take hold, grab you, and whisk you away. wrap themselves around you, soothe, tease, hold, and you get

sucked right in, lost in the simplicity and the gorgeousness of it all, until it hits you and you are left with the realization of how alone you are--how terribly and unmistakably alone--in the echoes of Phillip's words, there all along, to remind you." Marie Sabatino, Storyteller